MASTER NUMBERS

Cycles of Divine Order

Faith Javane

A Division of Schiffer Publishing
4880 Lower Valley Rd.
Atglen, PA 19310 USA

Master Numbers: Cycles of Divine Order

Copyright © 1988 by Faith Javane.
Library of Congress Catalog Number: 88-60422.

Cover design by Bob Boeberitz
Edited by Skye Alexander

Printed in China

ISBN: 0-914918-81-8

Published by Whitford Press
A Division of Schiffer Publishing, Ltd.
4880 Lower Valley Road
Atglen, PA 19310 USA
Phone: (610) 593-1777 Fax: (610) 593-2002
E-mail: Info@schifferbooks.com

In Europe, Schiffer books are distributed by Bushwood Books
6 Marksbury Avenue Kew Gardens
Surrey TW9 4JF England
Phone: 44 (0)208-392-8585; Fax: 44 (0)208-392-9876
E-mail: info@bushwoodbooks.co.uk
Free postage in the UK. Europe: air mail at cost.

Please visit our web site catalog at **www.schifferbooks.com** or write for a free catalog.
This book may be purchased from the publisher.
Please include $3.95 for shipping. Please try your bookstore first.
We are always looking for authors to write books on new and related subjects.
If you have an idea for a book please contact us at the address above.

Acknowledgments

Heartfelt acknowledgment and gratitude is lovingly expressed to Edith L. Harriman for her voluntary assistance in the preparation of the manuscript, which made the completion of this book much easier.

Loving thanks to Linda Stead, Joan Tilden, Carol Powel-Smith, and Linda Ward for their steady encouragement during the long time spent in preparation of this work.

Thanks to Shawn C. Harriman, whose editorial expertise provided many helpful suggestions.

And thanks to Joan Tilden for the symbolic diagrams.

Contents

Foreword

The aim of this book is to outline and delineate the journey of the soul. In the book I describe the soul's Divine creation, its descent into matter, its experiences in the Earth Plane, and its eventual evolution back to the Heaven World where it all began.

> "God said: 'Let us make man in our image.'"
> Genesis 1:26[1]

Many "paths" and "patterns of return" have been presented to us. This book employs the qualities and meanings in esoteric numerology as a presently understandable and ideal way of action for that "Path of Return."

My own introduction to numerology came in July of 1949, when I attended a course given in Boston by the internationally known teacher, Julia Seton, M.D. After class one day, Dr. Seton predicted to me, "Some day the time will come when all the double-digit master numbers will become active as we grow in consciousness to the point where our inner urges will increase, and higher and higher vibrations will be felt." She believed that the upper master numbers would offer opportunities for finer attainment toward Christ-hood as the human consciousness and soul unfoldment expanded.

Ever since 1949, I have thought of Dr. Seton's prophecy as I watched her forecast coming true. In response to the pressures of life's experiences, people of our time almost subconsciously have grown toward a wider vision. I also have looked for responses and indications within myself which might be interpreted as indicating that the time is now approaching when we must try to develop further a reasonable pattern of progression.

The science/art of numerology already has progressed significantly since Dr. Seton's time. In her practice, all double-digit numbers were promptly reduced to their single digits. Only the master numbers 11 and 22 were thoroughly delineated. The single-digit method was thus a greatly simplified system. Moreover, only the original five vowels (a, e, i, o, and u) were recognized. Today, the master numbers 33 and 44 have joined the list of activated numbers (meaning those whose vibrations have become active in our lives), as have all double-digits through the number 78 (thus paralleling the wisdom and philosophy in the seventy-eight tarot keys). Also, the letters "y" and in certain cases "w" have joined the other vowels in being considered active sacred letters. (See Appendix B for more discussion of this.) All this has greatly expanded the expression and meaning in numerology.

Hoping to contribute to this continuing expansion, I took up my pen to write down some ideas. My thoughts grew to such length that I have come to believe that I may have been "called" to author a book delineating some of the master numbers, the double-digit numbers that now seem to be producing responses in many people. I also decided to write further on all numbers containing the 11 because 11, the number of the planet Uranus, is called The Awakener. Since the discovery of Uranus in 1781, the consciousness of humankind has taken many strides forward, and numerology should recognize this and progress similarly. The resulting book has become particularly keyed to these upper esoteric vibrations, with their potential to serve those of advanced consciousness who will become the *Illuminati* of the future.

Note

1. All Biblical references are from the King James version.

Introduction

From the ancient Kabbalah to modern numerology the mystical import of numbers and letters, as symbols, has been significant in all sacred coded literature. Hidden meanings are discovered in many names, words, and phrases, or even as ideas within whole sentences when sacred writings are de-coded according to their numerological values. The Kabbalist knows how to de-code the esoteric meanings from Scripture, knows that this describes our inner soul life unity with God, and that it is the key to Cosmic harmony.

Tradition teaches that the material world is the visible aspect of the unseen world.

> The Lord made this world corresponding to the world above,
> and everything which is above has its counter-part below.

As above, so below. The central and most complete symbol between the above and below is the human being, made in God's Image.

> "And God said: 'Let us make man in our image.'"
> Genesis 1:26

"So God created man in his own image, in the image of God created he him, male and female created he them."
Genesis 1:27

Pictures, symbols, and numbers are understood in all languages. Esoteric numerology, esoteric astrology, and the spiritual philosophy pictured in the tarot keys are samples of God's "tools." They offer a quick, yet thorough way of analyzing and understanding ourselves.

My inquiring mind has made me a seeker after Truth. I probe for a reasonable explanation of life on Earth "as God's Image." The material I am offering may seem controversial to some, but to others may hold a reasonable and perhaps optimistic outlook. To me it is an outline of a possible pattern of evolution towards the "Image" we were created to manifest.

There are great Cosmic Patterns showing the important steps which lead to the upliftment of each of us to a point where union with the Higher Self is attainable. Perhaps the purpose of Earth evolution is to restore humanity to its full creative ability, working in harmony with the Divine Plan. There is a purpose behind the Universe, which the religions of all ages have known, and each has outlined a tentative spiritual path to super-consciousness. Eventually new world beliefs which will be a synthesis of the best plans of both East and West will be inaugurated.

Within the unending cycles of birth and death there must be profound meaning, even though we have not, as yet, come upon the seemingly inexplicable answer. We must push on to ever higher levels of harmony in Divine Order.

Science now confirms the awesome fact that we are all "Parts of one stupendous whole, whose body is Nature, and God the soul."

"In terms of both religion and science, modern thought no longer requires separation of matter and spirit — both are poles of one continuous living Universe."[1]
Roland Gammon

Nothing is more important for humankind to realize than the Oneness of all things, of time, of purpose, of effort. Although it may seem a vague concept, the oneness of all force is a basic truth. God, the first cause, the first principle, the first movement, "is, was, and ever shall be," the One Source that moves worlds, suns, stars, and whole solar systems in cycles of on-going creation.

Love and Law are one, even as the forces in nature are One. Each manifestation seeks to express that phase of its position given by its Creator. Only we humans abuse that position given, by our choices between good and evil. We may rise to become truly great in mastership, or we may regress many steps in character.

"Thou shalt have no other Gods before Me."
Deuteronomy 5:7

"Choose you this day whom you will serve."
Joshua 24:15

The study of ourselves in relation to the whole — or to God — and to the Oneness of all Force, will awaken something within our soul-selves to a full realization of the part we must play in future cycles of manifestation. To every individual a door is open, a new vision.

Spontaneous ideals and new thoughts and intuitions may bring higher dimensional experiences and speculations. At times, while we are reasoning through the conglomerate maze of Earth's vibrations, an original impulse can spark our imagination upon the universal cause and instant of creation.

We must admit and realize that the human kingdom is not an end in itself; it is only a bridge to a higher realm through illumination. Our spiritual growth must come from an inner search for fulfillment. The mind and heart must work together in perfect unison as life goes on in ever greater cycles of Divine Order. The influence of our hearts, minds, spirits, and wills is important in building our new finer bodies as instruments with possibilities of greater attainment. Evolution of conscious perception is bringing these changes in the awakening Aquarian Age. In order to meet the needs of our growing consciousness, we must go directly to the highest inspiration and creativity available — our own inner Being.

> "Within every human lies the potentialities of God-hood awaiting development and upliftment by the awakened operative 'I AM' within."[2]
>
> New Age Bible Interpretation

Evolution is as a spiral, and in each successive level a new "promised land" is brought into view.

> "Before man appeared upon Earth, he existed as a soul — as an astral Being and it was as such that he came to the physical world."[3]
>
> Rudolf Steiner

The story of humanity's evolution and the purpose of our unfolding powers is revealed by the hidden meaning of the number forces with which we are endowed. We incarnate bearing certain number symbols that are derived from our names and birthdates. These symbols point to a future state of illumination, our present status of evolution, and our ultimate destiny. Through positive response to these numbers — by visualizing and nurturing our inner guidance and by patient, careful, and steady effort — we can enjoy perfect peace and harmonious surroundings. A name or birthdate producing a power number gives boundless opportunity for improved self-expression. Those of us who incarnate under master numbers set the pace for coming advances in consciousness unfoldment, as their particular number symbols indicate.

> "Man's ultimate concern must be expressed symbolically, because symbolic language alone is able to express the ultimate."[4]
>
> Paul Tillich

When the master numbers become active as symbols in our lives, we develop the ability to create new conditions, new bodies, new lives, all in harmony with the Divine Image in whose likeness we have been made. These states of consciousness contribute to the birth of the Christ within each of us.

> "When correctly understood, the truths of the science of the spirit will give man a true foundation for his life, will let him recognize his value, his dignity and his essence — for these truths enlighten him about his connection with the world around him, they show him his highest goals, his true destiny."[5]
>
> Rudolf Steiner

When we have passed through many of the master number incarnations, we may be sure that some of them are recapitulations of work done in many former lifetimes.

From 0 to 100, we can build step by step, from animal to thinker, thinker to intellectual, intellectual to philosopher, philosopher to intuitionist, then by sublimation, to the Illuminati. Perhaps our Lord Jesus Christ became what we are that He might teach us what HE IS.

Notes

1. Roland Gammon, "Scientific Mysticism" *New Realities,* Vol. III, No. 6 (San Francisco: New Realities, Inc., 1980), pp. 8-14.

2. *New Age Bible Interpretation* Vol. I (Los Angeles: New Age Press, 1938), p. 190.

3. Rudolf Steiner, *Atlantis and Lemuria,* trans. Agnes Blake (London: Anthroposophical Publishing Co., 1923), p. 113.

4. Paul Tillich

5. Rudolf Steiner, *Cosmic Memory,* trans. K. E. Zimmer (New York: Harper & Row, Publishers, 1969), p. 249.

Part One

Prologue to the Journey

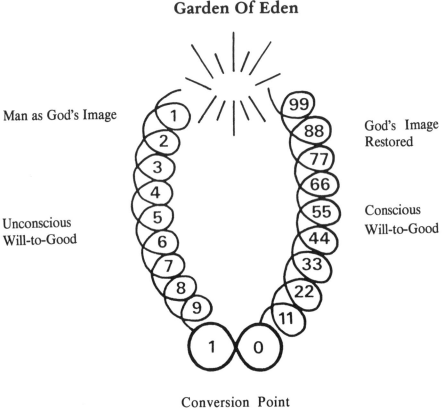

Will-To-Good
Garden Of Eden

Man as God's Image

Unconscious
Will-to-Good

God's Image
Restored

Conscious
Will-to-Good

Conversion Point
8654591956 76952
82/10

Chapter One

The Wisdom in the Symbol

All creation proceeds from Unity, and all manifested things must return and be received again into Unity. Herein is to be found the involutionary and evolutionary cycles of progression, both spiritual and material.

Corinne Heline

The spiral counterclockwise descent, subject to gravity, represents *involution*. The spiral clockwise ascent, observed as spirals of light, represents *evolution*.

Involution and evolution cover the journey of an Unconscious-Will-to-Good-Being to an individualized Conscious-Will-to-Good-Being with Universal Spirit . . . the human being. The conscious reunion of the oneness of all beings represents the passage from nescience to omniscience.

"Thou hast made us for Thyself, and the heart of man is restless until it finds itself in Thee."

St. Augustine

The symbol at left is a representation of the involutionary and evolutionary cycles of expression, both material and spiritual. It suggests that physical evolution exists in order to complete spiritual evolution, from the time of the soul's creation to its ultimate goal of Godhood, like a circling spiral taken one step at a time, moving ever upward to levels of greater awareness and oneness. The symbol shows the path leading to Godhood, from selfishness to altruism, and from desire to faith by way of the Divinity which is the Source of His Being.

> "The Earth is a training ground for the soul. All trials and tribulations may be experienced as a tempering of the soul so that it may move through into the eternal planes of higher consciousness."[1]
>
> George Trevelyan

All creation proceeds from unity to unity, and all manifested things must return to be resolved into unity. Teilhard de Chardin called this process, "homing upon the Omega Point" and knew that the Ultimate Being was the Divine Individual who said, "I AM Alpha and Omega, the first and the last." (Revelations 1:8)

Note

1. George Trevelyan, *Operation Redemption* (Wellingborough, England: Turnstone Press, Ltd., 1983), p. 19.

Chapter Two

Eons, Ages, Eras, Periods and Cycles

An eon is an immeasurably long period of time. An age is a division in historical time. An era is a division of time within an age. Periods and cycles refer to series of events coming in measured regularity.

Archaeologists have discovered much that enlightens us regarding deep antiquity. They have designated several important historical ages, including the Golden Age, the Silver Age, the Bronze Age, and the Iron Age. Occult scientists and those persons who consult the Akashic Records have proposed that each of these Ages covered thousands of years, based on modern science's findings that our Earth is much older than was formerly believed. The Ages describe developmental stages in our spiritual evolution. They are loosely comparable to stages in our actual historical record, but it is difficult to put even an approximate date to them that is satisfactory.

The Golden Age

The Golden Age represents a great cycle of time, possibly an eon, and it is believed to have been the Age of Truth. Gold, the most precious and brightest metal, was the symbol of the highest qualities of humanity. During this time only spiritual beings were present. Humanity was guided by Divine Will. Communication was accomplished by thought transference or telepathy. The Golden Age was a time of harmony, peace, and tranquility in which people spent their entire lives in wholeness and Oneness of Being. They were ideal creatures in purity and freedom, truly a race of immortals.

The term "primeval savage" is a familiar one in modern literature, but there is no evidence that the primeval savage ever existed. Rather, all the evidence points the other way. The mythical traditions of most cultures describe at the beginning of human history a time of happiness and perfection, a "Golden Age" which had no features of savagery or barbarism, but many of civilization and refinement.

It was stated in the Sibyline Prophecy that "When the Sun and Moon and Tishya (asterisms) and the planet Jupiter are in one mansion, the Golden Age shall return."[1]

The Silver Age

This age was another great wave of evolution involving thousands of years. Beings in the Silver Age were considered somewhat weaker spiritually than those who lived in the Golden Age. They were losing the keen awareness they formerly possessed. They had developed great pride in their intellect, which was an anathema to their Creator, and thus they began losing their "third eye vision," as well as becoming weaker in other spiritual qualities.

The Bronze Age

In this age many migrations occurred over the Earth. The beings living during this time had become more solidly flesh and more physically robust. Their five physical senses were active, but the spiritual world and direct communication with God were no longer available to them. Only a very few who wished to keep their consciousness above greed and violence retained this contact.

Violence erupted and warring took place for the first time on Earth. Men made weapons and armed themselves in bronze; they covered themselves from head to foot and spent their lives in fighting, calling themselves heros and warriors. This was a time of the awakening of the ego, or self-will. People had left the light and entered the darkness, becoming slaves to their senses, and worshippers of form and matter.

The Iron Age

The discovery of iron made possible the many machines, implements, and structures that are useful to us. The manufacture of weapons for warfare continued during this time, and more fearful and terrible machinations of violence intent on the conquest of whole nations took place. We are still in this Iron Age.

We know a great deal about the Taurean cycle within this Iron Age because that period was described extensively in the Bible. Each "cycle" within the Age lasts about two thousand years; therefore, a Great Age contains about twenty-four thousand years. During the Taurean cycle, idols such as the Golden Calf and the Bull were worshipped. The esoteric religion of that time was expressed through the opposite zodiacal sign Scorpio, and devotees of this religion were called "serpents of wisdom."

Biblical references to the Arien cycle, which followed the Taurean, tell of the "chosen people" and their Promised Land. The ram, symbol of Aries, and the "lamb of God" figured prominently in the lives of Abraham and Moses, described in the Old Testament, who lived during the Arien cycle. When Christ came, He was called the "Good Shepherd" and many of His teachings involved parables about shepherds and their sheep. For example, He told His disciples to "Feed my sheep — feed my lambs." (John 21:16)

The Iron Age is now finishing the cycle known as the Piscean Age. This cycle followed the Arien and began with the birth of Christ. Pisces' symbol is two fishes swimming in opposite directions, yet linked together. In the New Testament of the Bible, Jesus called His disciples "fishermen."Christ's teachings also included stories about fish, boats, and nets — all Piscean symbols. Early Christians used the fish as their symbol, before the cross became more prevalent. The esoteric symbols of Virgo, the sign opposite Pisces, are also prominent in stories about this time: the Virgin, purity, chastity, bread and wine, the harvest.

Now we are merging into the Aquarian Age. The sign Aquarius is associated with humanitarianism and altruism, and this cycle is expected to be a time when all people come together for the common good. Clairvoyance will become more prevalent as a means of communication. The spirit within us will become more active, and we can choose to work to purify our bodies, which in turn will make our thinking, feeling, and future hopes free from egotism. As this Piscean Age closes, people experiencing suffering and discontent will become more spiritual, approaching the goal of Christ Consciousness.

Note

1. H. P. Blavatsky, *The Secret Doctrine,* Vol. 5 (Wheaton, IL: Theosophical University Press, 1946), p. 339. ("Asterism" denotes a cluster of stars. "Mansion" refers to a zodiacal sign.This may be a reference to Tsha or Ampelos, a star at 15 degrees of Virgo.)

Chapter Three

The Garden of Eden

*So God created man in His own Image, in the Image of God
created He him, male and female created He them.*
Genesis 1:27

In the Garden of Eden, we, the Soul-Selves, were created in God's
Image. Thus the "fall" represents the integration of Spirit with matter
in the Earth plane through the physical body. Here, each of us made
the decision to pursue our own separate paths, using our own wills and
power. Our problem became to re-learn how to control the Creative
Power.

Our incarnation produced the realization of Being — the consciousness of "I AM" — an awakening, as the life-energy worked on
our minds to help us become aware of the higher spirals of consciousness
yet to be attained.

"One's earthly career was already determined the very moment he fell out of Divine Unity for the first time, just as a
boomerang, at the moment it is thrown, has within itself the
forces that determine the kind of circle it will make — and
when it will return to its starting point."[1]
Elizabeth Haich

The theme "from darkness to light" covers involution into matter and evolution to the Spiritual Kingdom. This process has lasted eons of time and requires countless incarnations in the flesh for attainment. Evolution back to our spiritual home demands that we become truly self-less, and have a willingness to serve others. We have been a long time finding out why we are here on Earth and for what purpose we needed to experience the human kingdom.

> "When the eyes of the body were opened the sight of the soul was obscured."[2]
>
> Manly P. Hall

It seems clear that we were intended to use this power to create in the Image of God through the spiritualization and perfect blending of the separated sexes. When this great lesson is learned, we will be allowed to "eat of the tree of life" and "become as one of us." (Genesis 3:22)

> "Anthropology submits evidence proving the ascent of man, orthodox religion teaches the fall of man. Occultism reconciles the two."[3]
>
> New Age Bible Interpretation

Knowledge of truth in the Tree of Life is not gained until we have finished the experience in the lesser polarities, for it is necessary to finish our course by progressing out of the negative states of Earth consciousness. To regain the love and truth consciousness, we have much to learn about good and evil, and when it is known it is not condemned, but understood. Truth reveals that love is finally regained more through pain and suffering than through pleasure.

The "self" is not only a body, but is a non-physical mind, a soul mind. True wisdom lies concealed in every cell in our bodies, as our God-self within. In the outside world we see a mass of contradictions and conflicts. To find the answers our souls are seeking, we must turn within. Thus, we come to realize that our "self" is identical with the God-Self. The mind must listen to the Spirit within, in order to awaken and hear the promise: "I, God, shall be with you the minute you speak to Me." (Isaiah 66:24)

We live in three-dimensional bodies, but we know of existence in other dimensions. What in us knows? The Soul consciousness!

"Man is not the body, but a non-physical mind, a center of consciousness, a personality, a conscious self, a soul."[4]
Benito F. Reyes

The Bible teaches that we are eternal beings; thus, our consciousness extends beyond this Piscean Age into ages beyond, and to the fourth, fifth, sixth, seventh, and eighth dimensions in consciousness.

"This Solar System has at least Eight dimensions of consciousness. Each and every entity passes through the spheres, or planes, of every planet:

3rd dimension - Earth - Three dimensions
4th dimension - Venus - Love, forgiveness
5th dimension - Jupiter - Spiritual consciousness
6th dimension - Uranus - Occult, psychic
7th dimension - Neptune - Mystic revelations
8th dimension - Pluto - Redemptive, transcendental"[5]
Edgar Cayce

Spirit supersedes the mind, which tells us to declare our faith openly, for God's eye is ever on those who love Him. When we have learned the truth about the self and live according to our beliefs, we have chosen the path of fulfillment. We must forgive all and love all if we would have our prayers answered. By prayer and by faith we learn the words of truth — faith to penetrate, to see and feel beyond illusion, through all the "fire" of testing, faith to know that we must climb, and do and dare, and reach up through the spiral ladder of hope, and obey the "Will-to-be." Only by patience and spiral growth can these things fulfill our goal.

Human consciousness is a developing thing. Mystical consciousness represents a higher stage than has been reached at our present time in evolution.There are deeper latent powers of mind yet to be found and utilized. In the new Age of Aquarius there will emerge a higher level of unfolding consciousness, merging toward an ultimate reality of peace. An enormous field for investigation stretches ahead in ages to come for all who care to explore other realms of consciousness.

A sense of Deity in us drives us forward from the most primitive experience and adventure to the great work of building the pathway of light from the dense material world to the spiritual one. This brings an awe-inspiring surge for peace, sweeping over the total humanity in the coming millennia.

The German theologian, Meister Eckhart (1250-1327) taught that "God must become I, and I must become God."[6] Eckhart believed that God and the human being could be united because they were already One, truly Divine Beings: God, the Father, and man, the son.

Love, Divinity, and Will, united spiritually, produce wisdom. Our spiritual Comforter and Inspirer came to Earth to enlighten reverent and humble souls to new levels of consciousness, and thus to new vistas of understanding.

"Man shall discover the secret of Life as he explores Light."[7]
The Golden Scripts

The ancients believed light to be Holy. Jesus taught that Light is Truth, and called His disciples "children of Light." (John 12:36) "While ye have Light, believe in the Light, that ye may be called Children of Light." (1 Thessalonians 5:5) "But now ye are Light in the Lord, walk as children of Light." (Ephesians 5:8)

We can choose to tune in, and remain in, the flow of Divine Order in all our activities and in every moment of our lives. Divine Order is active in our lives. It brings change that inspires us to grow and discover new abilities within ourselves, which leads us to rise to the ultimate goal of enlightenment.

"Involution always precedes evolution. The 'I AM' and its spiritual faculties must be sent down into the body-consciousness before the evolution of the spiritual man can begin."[8]

Charles Fillmore

Notes

1. Elizabeth Haich, *Initiation* (London: George Allen and Unwin, Ltd., 1965), p. 271.

2. Manly P. Hall, *The Mystical Christ* (LA: The Philosophical Research Society, Inc., 1956), p. 127.

3. *New Age Bible Interpretation,* Vol. I (Los Angeles: New Age Press, 1938), p. 20.

4. Benito F. Reyes, *The Scientific Proofs of the Existence of the Soul* (Manila, Philippines: Lotus Press, 1949), p. 67.

5. Edgar Cayce, *The Readings* (Virginia Beach, VA: Association for Research and Enlightenment, Inc.), reading 254-27.

6. Meister Eckhart

7. *The Golden Scripts* (Noblesville, IN: Soulcraft Chapels, 1951), p. 202.

8. Charles Fillmore, *Mysteries of Genesis* (Kansas City, MO: Unity School of Christianity, 1952), p. 323.

Chapter Four

The New Golden Age

Consider the Earth's position in the Cosmos. Astronomy tells us that our solar system is located within the Milky Way Galaxy, and that the solar system is under a golden Sun's radiation. This radiation is creating a higher frequency vibration, affecting our solar system and all life on the planet Earth. It will be felt physically, mentally, and spiritually by all.

This change will endure for many years, and will gradually make us more aware of the future possibilities in our society. The incoming souls who incarnate during this time will not be resistant to spiritual ethics. Extra-sensory perception (E.S.P.) and telepathy, as well as clairvoyance and clairaudience, will become the norm. These incoming egos will be of higher quality and will take charge of our planet. The Earth undergoes changes through long periods of time called "ages." Oceans become lands, and lands, oceans. This is necessary for the cosmic purification of the planet. When the land lies under saltwater for hundreds of years, it becomes purified for future habitation. Thus, the "school room" Earth is renovated and made ready for new students.

The new vibrations may be felt more by those who are spiritually developed, and those who resist change may not be able to endure the altitudes of the higher vibrations. Let us not fear these events to come, but remember the prophecies which refer to the glorious new ages when our hopes and ideals will be realized.

The Importance of Love

Intellectual understanding alone will never teach us about the inner spiritual laws of life. Until we learn to live the life of love, good-will, and forgiveness, our hearts will experience a hunger for peace and harmony. Many seek the esoteric teachings and desire to know the inner mystery of God, which in one word, is LOVE.

Psychological research has determined that love engenders extraordinary longevity and vigorous health. Only love can dissolve hate, fear, and desire for revenge. Fear dims the guiding light we need to help us attain the higher consciousness. Acts of love develop faith. We must have faith that the Lord loves us, and will forgive us, no matter what! All that is required is repentance while obeying the admonition, "Go and sin no more." (John 8:11)

Within each of us there is vast creative potential. We mature quite naturally physically and psychologically; we gradually realize that we are creating a new culture. This realization is the emergence of the Divine, like a living spirit of unfoldment within. Psychiatry and religion have come to the same conclusion — we must love our neighbors in order to survive, and when we mistreat others, we operate against the Holy Spirit.

The only subject that should be claiming our interest is the soul. If we still incarnate in Earth, then "school" is not yet finished for us; we still need to learn obedience to the immutable laws of love. Will power will carry us far, but only love can keep us safe and help our souls to unfold.

The way of love is the way of perfect faith. What the mind dwells upon is very sure to manifest itself. Every thought and feeling that flows through us qualifies our actions. We are creating either harmony or discord, even now, day by day. We sow and reap; action and reaction resonate throughout the Universe.

Our present form of civilization is ending. Not everything will pass on at once, but our ways of living are changing. New customs are taking place in birthing, relating, and even in the care of the dead.

The ideal of every spiritual system of unfoldment is to find a perfect pattern for continued growth and development. When we think of all the wonders to come when humankind pursues its holistic talents, we can conceive of a new Golden Age as a reality. The regaining of the Golden Age means that the gold of Divine Love will permeate souls and love between all peoples will become an actuality here on Earth.

Chapter Five
Esoteric Numerology

The spiritual significance and orderly progression of all manifestation can be clearly understood by way of the art and science of Esoteric
Numerology. Spiritual growth can be approached from many angles;
however, we will delineate herein by using the qualities, attributes, and
relationships as shown through number symbology.

Although we all have names and birthdates, few people know of
the mysteries and qualities of consciousness expressed within when our
names and birthdates are reduced to their number vibrations. These
also reveal our particular status and cosmic gifts and tell us plainly
where we stand in power or weakness.

> "All beings . . . down to the lowest atomic existence have their
> particular numbers, which distinguishes each from the other,
> and becomes the source of their attributes and qualities of
> their destiny."[1]

H. P. Blavatsky

All peoples, even the most primitive, have shown some insight and fa-
miliarity with numbers. The basic vibrations derived from our names
and birthdates faithfully describe our true natures and dispositions, and

represent the energy patterns received by us upon taking our first breaths. It is valuable to our understanding to study and meditate upon our own numbers. They foretell our mission in life and point to our possibilities for accomplishment. Our numbers are the indices of our talents and potentials. When we have learned to understand ourselves and found how to interpret our numbers, our lives will be happier and we will have a new purpose for living. We will have discovered the particular lessons for our present incarnations were taken and thus, can concentrate on mastering them. (See Appendix A: Finding Your Numbers in Esoteric Numerology.)

It is believed that the sum-total of all knowledge existent in the Universe is penetrable by the mind that is competent to lift its own vibration high enough to reach this knowledge.

Apropos to the beginnings of the numberings, the following verses excerpted from the 85th chapter of *The Golden Scripts* seem helpful to our understanding.

Verses

1 - 3 Numbers express values — they teach the most profound study in all creation.

10 When man first came to earth, he had knowledge of himself as One, he had knowledge of his neighbor which made Two and he had many neighbors which made many numbers.

The Zero

In esoteric numerology, Zero is classified as a number. It stands for all that was before creation; therefore, it stands for God, pure Spirit, Divine Light, the All, the Absolute, the Living Light, Creative Power, That which Was, Is, and Shall Be. It is also described as Omniscient Deity, First Cause, the I AM, the All-Seeing-Eye, Fountain of Eternal

Life, the Will-To-Good, Super-Consciousness, Protection, Perfection, and Love.

The Zero does not add or subtract qualities in a situation, but is redemptive, as it raises the qualities by a Power; for example, 1 is raised to 10, 2 to 20, 3 to 30, and so forth. People whose name or birthdate numbers are expressed as digits plus the Zero (e.g., 10, 20, 30) show much initiative. They go forward with confidence because of the protection and Divine Consciousness of the Zero.

> "Ye have labor to perform beyond earthly understanding —
> seeking a way to accomplish their Divine Missions."[3]
> The Golden Scripts

Cyclic progression is the theme of all life. We are reminded of the Biblical story of Jacob, who, after he had lived by faith in God in the higher consciousness, was told, "Thy Name shall no more be called Jacob, but Israel." (Genesis 32:28)

JACOB	ISRAEL
11362	919153
13/4	28/10
(a four-powered name)	(a ten-powered name)

> "Numbers are the elements of a sublime theological symbolism."[4] a fragment of genuine Pythagorean onomanics.

> "1 + 2 + 3 + 4 = 10 was his way of expressing this idea. The ONE is God . . . The TWO is matter . . . the THREE, combining Monad and Duad and partaking of the nature of both, is the phenomenal world, the Tetrad or form of perfection. The Decad, or sum of all . . . involves the entire cosmos."[5]

> "The Decad is the world which receives the images of all the Divine Numbers which are supernally imparted to it. The Decad was called Heaven from being the most perfect boundary

of number . . . as Heaven is the receptacle of all things. As the Decad contains every Number in itself, and the Number is infinite, perhaps it was on this account called Eternity — for Eternity is Infinite Life."[6]

Thomas Taylor

Notes

1. H. P. Blavatsky, *The Secret Doctrine,* Vol. 5 (Wheaton, IL: Theosophical University Press, 1946), p. 116.

2. *The Golden Scripts* (Noblesville, IN: Soulcraft Chapels, 1951), chapter 85.

3. Ibid., 49:70, p. 192.

4. Thomas Taylor, *Theoretic Arithmetic of the Pythagoreans* (New York: Samuel Weiser, Inc., 1975), p. vii.

5. Ibid., p. 207.

6. Ibid., pp. 205-206.

Part Two
The Soul's Journey

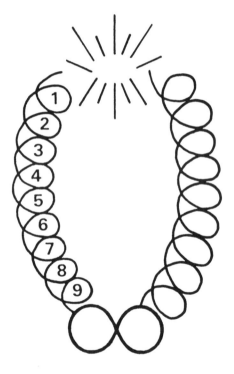

Chapter Six

Through the Digits

T he souls, having left the Garden of Eden by their own choice, came into bodily incarnation on the Earth Plane as individual male and female entities. An innocent soul comes into physical manifestation completely forgetting its origin, yet bearing within itself the first great Divine Aspect, the Will-To-Good, the hidden I AM consciousness. An occult aphorism states, "Matter is spirit at its lowest point of manifestation, and Spirit is matter at its highest state."

One: The Masculine Principle

Number One individuals, that is, those whose names or birthdates add together and reduce to the number One, need to understand who they are, for they are to become "trail blazers." They are the first to achieve self-consciousness, the first to say, "I AM."

ADAM	EVA[1]	PIONEER	FRONT	BEING
1414	541	7965559	69652	25957
10/1	10/1	46/1	28/1	28/1

These pioneers must learn to visualize and to do many untried actions in materiality; they have to accustom themselves to their elemental environment. They learn to anticipate results through trial and error. Their imaginations soar, but without tangible results because of their inexperience. Without knowing why, they desire to be leaders. They want to be at the front. They will advance to become commanders-in-chief, or to be people who stand alone simply on their convictions. They want to dominate because they think of themselves as the center of their world.

They must learn that life does not unfold all at once — they must find true being, and express it. Each of them is the microcosm and now must struggle to understand the macrocosm.

The Need: Learn to stand on your own feet, and develop independence.

Two: The Feminine Principle

The "me and not me," the "mine and not mine" is reflected in the number Two. Patience, endurance, and consideration for others are attributes which are to be learned while under this number. "What I have and do not have" is a lesson in safety and security, to be learned under the Two. The use of free will has taught number Two people tact and caution. By becoming peacemakers or "go-betweens" they will heal many wounds of pride and be constructive workers in the world. These people cultivate peaceful co-existence. Through time, toil, and the will to become successful world citizens they will be able to balance the duality inherent in this number.

TIME	TOIL	WILL	DUALITY	BALANCE
2945	2693	5933	4313927	2131535
20/2	20/2	20/2	29/11/2	20/2

Cosmic Love is an attracting, fusing, cohesive force, moving toward Oneness. Harmony, which is a type of Cosmic Love inherent in us all, will endure until all may become as One, though diversified in consciousness.

The number Two represents all pairs of opposites: male-female, Spirit-matter, youth-age, Mars-Venus, fertile-barren, pain-pleasure, etc. Each demonstrates the "law of attraction," which develops the needed characteristic of diplomacy.

Patience and endurance are attributes learned in the number Two experience.

The Ideal: To work for harmony in relationships.

Three

The growing cycle is now manifesting in the Trinity: $1 + 2 = 3$. Three people must learn to think and concentrate, to specialize and not scatter energy. They must be able to express creative faculties, to harmonize their energies with their emotions, and to develop diversified personalities. They must seek to expand and grow in judgment, to analyze in preparation for future events. The intelligence of Threes becomes active and energetic; they learn how to go forward with expanded plans for their chosen goals. They are aware of their bodies as instruments for providing delight and satisfaction.

GROWING	CYCLE	ANALYZE	MEDIATE	TOLERANCE
7965957	37335	1513785	4549125	263591535
48/3	21/3	30/3	30/3	39/3

This is a stage of progressive development through multiple experiences, experiences both of success and failure. Three people learn what to do and what not to do. They become ready to organize their time efficiently. Trinities are like forerunners of ultimate perfection and triumph. These primodial Threes are aspects of conditions to appear in the future, but are first concerned with the process of growth.

Father-Mother-Child   Father-Son-Holy Spirit

Spirit, life, and energy express themselves as form, individuality, and self-consciousness, finally completing the knowledge of Soul Consciousness and Light, or Super-consciousness.When the Three experience is absorbed in consciousness, Three individuals may become happy geniuses.

```
HAPPY          GENIUS
81777          755931
30/3           30/3
```

The Urge: To conserve the growing faith in yourself while encouraging others to expand theirs as well.

Four

The soul now awakens as a number Four type individual. These people have the potential to seek and find work which will be constructive for their futures. Their reputations now are being built on honesty and practicality.

Number Four persons are believers in law, system, and order. They can be depended upon to do faithful work, executed in a most conscientious way, and often are promoted to management positions. These people assume responsibility well and build security at the same time.

Number Four personalities maintain and carry out plans and formulas; they make ideas concrete and workable. These individuals start undertakings that require patience, perseverence, and determination, and the urge to affect outstanding results.

```
SEEK    WORK    PATIENT    POTENTIAL
1552    5692    7129552    762552913
13/4    22/4    31/4       40/4
```

Number Four individuals have high standards of honesty, and they perform faithful work. They glory in accomplishments and are well regarded by contemporaries. They have a stabilizing quality and can organize their time so as to succeed in all their projects.

Fours are loyalty personified, constructing their futures in a conservative way, always building for permanence. Their secret of success is affability, and being able to give to friends and associates as they would like to receive. Keywords for a Four personality are "steadfastness" and "endurance."

The Purpose: To share knowledge and wisdom.

Five

The energy of Five is intelligence. It is the inherent will-to-know and to be the "I AM!"

Five personalities enjoy change and travel. They cannot endure a dull existence or a monotonous, tedious type of work, but must anticipate challenge to accomplish the seemingly impossible. They learn easily and are unafraid of testing the new and untried. They are efficient, flexible, and can adapt well to most circumstances. The law of the Five is freedom in action. Fives are clever, versatile, and skilled. They will say, "Don't fence me in" and "I can do that and more."

RESEARCH	EXPLORER	LEARN	EXPERIENCE	JOY
95151938	56736959	35195	5675995535	167
41/5	50/5	23/5	59/5	14/5

Number Five people have mental dexterity, and great ability to learn, talk, sell, promote, and teach. They want variety, adventure, and excitement. They desire to be explorers and to experience the joys of living.

SUBSTANCE	LIFE
132121535	3965
23/5	23/5

A great and inspiring goal of Five individuals would be the regeneration of the body through control of the senses. The will of the Five is inherent in substance, and the energy is that of liberation.

The nature of Fives is restlessness; their consuming curiosity leads them to try to be part of everything within their environment, and thus to know what is going on in the world. They make interesting compan-

ions; life is never dull when they are present.
    Change is the keynote of all Fives.

The Focus: To attain greater stability.

Six

Number Six individuals may regain the sixth sense — intuition. They
are artistic and love peace and harmony. They could do well in careers
in social services because their understanding leads to justice and compassion.

TRUTH	JUSTICE	UNDERSTANDING	COMPASSIONATE
29328	1312935	3545912154957	3647111965125
24/6	24/6	60/6	51/6

Sixes love animals and are sympathetic towards them. All of nature
is their primary concern; thus, they could become naturalists. They
have keen understanding of the Earth and seek to protect it. Number
Six people may express this innate connection with the Earth through
gardening, landscaping, and other fields that utilize nature's beauty.
Their homes, families, and friends are also of prime importance.
    Fastidious and discriminating, Six people are usually cheerful,
kind and accommodating. Their appreciation of beauty could incline
them toward artistic pursuits.

ARTIST	WORD
192912	5694
24/6	24/6

The number Six embodies the essence of devotion and idealism. Its love
energy, expressed through humanity in a unique manner, is related to
the Will-to-Good and has a vague, or inner, recognition of a Divine
Plan. Six individuals desire to follow this Plan and they interpret it as
a way of service; but, they must be careful not to let others lean on them
to the detriment of themselves or others. Self-sacrifice is ideal but it
must be balanced.

The Vision: Identification with Christ-like qualities.

Seven

The quality of each cell in our physical bodies is determined by the character of our thoughts. "As a man thinketh in his heart so is he." (Proverbs 23:7)

Humankind is a physical vehicle of thought, feeling, and action. Number Seven individuals are challenged to heed their inner guidance. This incarnation, as a Seven, could represent the "step" where this person passes from the mundane to the more sensitive, or soul-like consciousness.

In the Seven position, people can visualize their goals and focus on the ideals they want to attain in the future. This is the time when they cultivate faith in the justice of God's cycles of Divine Order. Seven individuals may wish to become Apostles of a beloved Adept, or to train and study to enter the Clergy. Seven is the number of the potential mystic. These people are interested in phenomena, the curious, the inexplicable, and the super-natural. They realize there is something over and above the material or mundane consciousness, as they sometimes contact the etheric forces, and — without realizing how — they bring forth profound truths that can benefit the world.

CLERGY	APOSTLE	HEART	SELF-SACRIFICE		GRACE
335977	1761235	85192	1536	113996935	79135
34/7	25/7	25/7	61/7		25/7

Number Seven people will diligently study these Seven Messages of Mysticism:

1. The Principle of Mentalism. All is mind;
2. The Principle of Correspondence. As above, so below;
3. The Principle of Vibration. Nothing rests. Everything moves;
4. The Principle of Polarity. Everything is dual, pairs;
5. The Principle of Rhythm. Everything flows. Tides come in and out;

6. The Principle of Cause and Effect. Each cause has its effect;
7. The Principle of Gender. Gender manifests on all planes.[2]

Seven individuals have integrity and are careful to fulfill any trust assigned to them. Their strong intuition helps them to choose the best and most advantageous answer to most problems in life. Seven people are very keen and sensitive, often misunderstood — sometimes enigmas even to themselves. At times they make their friends uneasy by seeing right through their outer personalities, but Sevens are always well-meaning for they are really seeking spiritual progress.

The Prayer: Be still, and know that I AM GOD.

Eight

Aspirants, having experienced the learning processes from number One through number Seven, now incarnate as number Eights. They are pleased with their progress and feel that they are ready for that "something more" that they glimpsed as number Sevens. A sense of power thrills through every fiber of their beings. They drive themselves toward goals that are beyond where they have been before.

They think in terms of success and prosperity. Number Eight people are responsible workers, and their employers and co-workers trust and believe in their integrity. They are systematic and methodical, and generally use wise and practical judgment.

GOAL	SUCCESS	PROSPERITY	RESPONSIBLE	TRUST
7613	1333511	7961759927	95176519235	29312
17/8	17/8	62/8	53/8	17/8

Eight individuals aspire to be executives or owners of the prosperous businesses where they began as underlings. They work to reach the top in their professions and particularly like big business and high finances. Ambitious, they strive for status and power.

MOSES	FAITH	HOPE	ADEPTSHIP	GOD
46151	61928	8675	145721897	764
17/8	26/8	26/8	44/8	17/8

Moses, a man of power, led the Israelites out of Egypt. His name was a positive influence of strength for leadership. Number Eight people have faith and hope that they may attain adeptship by pursuing the Divine Plan and obeying God. They mediate on re-opening the "third eye" and strive to keep the channels clear for realization of their spiritual goals for this lifetime.

The Goal: To awaken the Divinity within.

Nine

Nine individuals serve others. They express benevolence toward comrades in such a way that it brings out the best qualities in them. Nines are growing in clemency, tolerance, forgiveness, and understanding, which will help them to reap the fullness of their potential. As they awaken, their inner knowing consumes all the dross of self-centeredness.

INNER	KNOWING	THOUGHT	SERVICE	HUMILITY
95559	2565957	2863782	1594935	83493927
72/9		36/9	36/9	45/9

By respecting the Law of Love and Service, and by practicing humility, number Nine individuals can turn passion into compassion. They grow in fidelity as they use their talent to become whole.

PASSION	TO	COMPASSION	FIDELITY	WHOLE	LOVE
7111965	26	3647111965	69453927	58635	3645
81/9			45/9	27/9	18/9

An ancient wisdom mantra declares, "One may have all knowledge, yet if he does not have love, he does not possess a single letter of the alphabet of true wisdom." The letter is "YOD," a flame-like symbol, and tenth letter of the so-called sacred Hebrew Alphabet.

```
DIVINE TIMING
494955 294957
72/9
```

Education, science, or statesmanship can be the forte of number Nine individuals. They have confidence in themselves, faith in the order of Divine Timing, and love for their fellow beings. Nine is the number of universality, love, and understanding. This is

```
THE HUMANITARIAN
285 834159219915
72/9
```

People whose names or birthdates are single digit numbers (1 through 9) are primarily learners who like to investigate and experiment. Nine contains the potency of all previous learning situations. A complete cycle of growth has been attained.These individuals have come "full circle" (360 degrees: 3 + 6 + 0 = 9) and now are motivated to take the next step of understanding self in relation to God. Their foresight goes beyond the present, their next step being the introduction of the 1 plus the 0, or the first double digit:10. To whom much is given, much is also expected.

The Hope: To create new foundations for further growth on higher octaves.

Notes

1. Eva was the name used in early Biblical manuscripts.
2. Three Initiates, *The Kybalion: Hermetic Philosophy* (Chicago: Yogi Publication Society, 1912), pp. 25-26.

Chapter Seven

The Conversion Point

Ten is the first digit with the Zero in the scale of vibrations. This endows individuals whose names or birthdate numbers are Ten with extra vitality. They may use this vitality to earn the crown of attainment and to maintain the symbol of wholeness.

VITALITY	CROWN	MAN
49213927	39655	415
37/10	28/10	10

The number Ten represents the point of conversion, when people see themselves as upright beings, pioneers. They have learned to handle all the powers of leadership and judgment. They begin to realize that standing with them, even within themselves, is the whole God-power of the Universe. At this point they make a decision: "I must arise and go to my Father." (Luke 15:18), and hear within themselves: "Arise — Shine — for the Light is come." (Isaiah 60:1)

ARISE	SHINE	LIGHT
19915	18955	39782
25/7	28/10	29/11

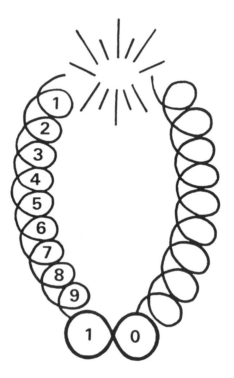

The number Seven means "soul progress." The number Ten means "conversion." The number Eleven corresponds to "mastership." The individual is now inspired to take the following steps to do the Great Work, to walk the Path of Evolution toward immortality. There are ten stages of mind unfoldment — plus one.

1. Instinct
2. Sensed thinking
3. Reasoning
4. Mind thinking
5. Mind knowing
6. Mind imagining
7. Intuition
8. Inspiration
9. Creative attitudes
10. Cosmic Consciousness
    (plus 1 = 11)
11. Illumination

The number 10 is a symbol of wholeness, humanity (1) and God (0) in unity, the great gift of power and protection. Number Ten people must use their boundless energy for promoting their "Will-To-Good" and seeking to carry out their paramount mission.

```
PARAMOUNT MISSION        CONVERSION POINT
719146352 4911965        3654591965 76952
73/10                    82/10
```

They are beginning new lessons in cycles of knowledge. As the life energy works through their minds, they develop a higher spiral in consciousness. All forms of life exist as extensions, or as universal cycles of orderly growth. Great responsibility rests on number Ten individuals. Having reached the conversion point, they must now use their strong will power to undergo the discipline necessary to prepare for the coming Aquarian Age, where they will need to cope with new discoveries.

```
STRONG WILL POWER       DISCIPLINE        AQUARIAN
129657 5933 76559       4913973955        18319915
82/10                   55/10             37/10
```

Spiritual science becomes the bridge between the faith of the Piscean Age and the electronics of the Aquarian Age. Ten individuals have come into a strata of consciousness with new ideals and new inventions to be controlled.

"The open mind is the gateway to philosophy."
Plato

The Incentive: To keep the flow of Spiritual Light in steady operation.

Chapter Eight

Special Numbers

Certain numbers between 10 and 20 are unique and require more explanation and attention. These are the Special Numbers: 12, 13, 14, 16, and 19. (Number 11 is covered under Master Numbers.)

Twelve

The number Twelve represents a complete cycle of experience; thus, it is not strange that in the Bible both the Old and New Testaments often use this number symbolically. For example, the twelve sons of Jacob in the Old Testament became known as the Twelve Tribes of Israel. Each tribe represented characteristic numerical and zodiacal attributes that were to be awakened and developed within them. Each tribe was given a blessing for guidance and leadership (Jacob's blessing in Genesis 49:1-28). Those of the Tribe of Levi were designated as the spiritual leaders for all the tribes, and Aaron, a Levite, became the first priest. In honor of his position, he wore a breast-plate of twelve precious stones set in gold, identified with the names of the tribes, and used as an oracular "urim and thummim" by which he could determine the Divine Will to attain judgments and settle disputes for the good of the people. These spiritual leaders often had to advise a "reversal of conduct" for their followers, requiring different evolving lifestyles for their spiritual growth.

Let us consider the diagram below of the Breast-plate of Aaron, as described in Exodus 28:15-30, and examine the traditional meanings of the twelve stones.

			Stone	*Meaning*
Sardius	Topaz	Carbunkle	Sardius Topaz Carbunkle	Stability Faith Charity
Emerald	Sapphire	Diamond	Emerald Sapphire Diamond	Fidelity Peace Victory
Ligure	Agate	Amethyst	Ligure (a form of ruby) Agate Amethyst	Justice Courage Love
Beryl	Onyx	Jasper	Beryl Onyx Jasper	Modesty Moral Integrity Truth, Safety

In the New Testament, Jesus repeated this symbolic theme by choosing twelve apostles. The Apostles also represented characteristic numerical and zodiacal attributes to be used for the good of the people. Thus, Jesus had a complete and representative inner circle, a cross section of the people of those times as disciples to receive His teachings.

When individuals enter incarnation as number Twelves they have had a full cycle of experience and learned of the possibility of regeneration toward a higher consciousness. They belong to the group of developed souls who have accumulated unusual inner strength through many and varied experiences from many lifetimes in the flesh. However, these people still may be hindered by old habits that need to be changed. The soul attracts that which it needs as a learning experience. A *reversal* of negative thoughts can bring about positive effects and aid in achieving ideal goals or aspirations. If challenged, the number Twelve person's initial response might be, "Why me?" Instead they should think, "Why not me?"

For instance, people may be poor but very anxious to improve their surroundings and home comforts, yet they shirk work and consider themselves justified because they are poorly paid. They do not understand the principle of prosperity, which calls for honest and fair work by doing one's best wherever one may be. Or, an employer may engage in devious measures to avoid paying employees adequately in hopes of making a larger profit. Such individuals are unfit for prosperity; they usually blame their ill-luck on others, rather than on their own selfish thinking. In each case, the "Law of Reversal" would correct the situation.

The Cue: Reversal.

Thirteen

The number Thirteen is often considered an unlucky number, perhaps because it has been called the number of death. Many people do not realize that it refers not to physical death, but rather to the mystical death of old, worn-out ideas and circumstances. It represents those who have been reborn through their mental powers of transmutation; therefore, Thirteen is a sacred number.

We can think of the number Thirteen in three ways: as generation (creativity), degeneration (a "fall" from grace), or regeneration (the attaining of higher consciousness). With these considerations, it behooves number Thirteen individuals to strive to transmute all their "vices" into "virtues." They must act squarely and be just, merciful, and moral to attain victory for their higher soul selves. Number Thirteen people go through trials, tests, and temptations in their search for a way to the greater life of spiritual consciousness. Their consciences must always be their guides. They must seek more Light.

FALL	SOUL	WAY	SEEK
6133	1633	517	1552
13	13	13	13

The number Thirteen is more spiritual than the Four (the single-digit number to which 1 + 3 add) because the higher octave numbers have greater power vibrations that can be used for the benefit of others. Thirteen individuals are called upon to sacrifice self for others and for the eventual good of all humanity. Thirteen is a number of wisdom and right judgment. Spiritual growth more often is attained through pain than through pleasure.

These meanings might account for number Thirteen's being called unlucky. However, it is only considered unlucky by those who do not understand.

The Seeking: The Better Way.

Fourteen

People born under the number Fourteen must learn independence, self-initiative, unity, and justice. Their need is to achieve balance, harmony, temperance, and prudence. If they act cautiously they can be fortunate in dealings with money and speculation, or changes in business.

The number Fourteen has been considered a malefic, a number that can have strong negative influence on people unless they are awake and aware of conditions which come into their lives. At times they will feel determined, even downright stubborn, about having their way. The free spirituality of the underlying Five (1 + 4 = 5) seems to be overpowered.

AWAKE	FATE	JOY	AIM
15125	6125	167	194
14	14	14	14

In analyzing your numbers, you must be watchful for the number Fourteen. If it occurs in your Soul Number, it indicates an immersion in the sensational in the past. If it is found in your Personality Number, watch physical appetites in the present, for if temptations to over-indulgences are gratified, the outcome could bring destruction to the physical vehicle (body), because the Fourteen denotes a physical "fall" of some kind.

The number Fourteen is one of everlasting movement, and brings trials and dangers from the great variety of experiences. These people sometimes experiment for the sake of experience. Such behavior may lead to chaos, but their aim is to try for progressive change and the final joy of renewal and growth.

To the ancients the number Fourteen meant enlightenment. To them, Fourteen stood for gold, the "gold of enlightenment" or verified truth. Thus, if the Fourteen individual's aims are kept high, the result is reward and profit.

The Watching: Urges may be harmful to your purpose.

Sixteen

Number Sixteen people must keep their feet upon the "path of higher spiritual learning." They must cultivate willpower, initiative, and independent action to help overcome obstacles that can come into this experience, for Sixteen is another of the so-called malefic numbers. It most often works through the emotions.

As a malefic, the number Sixteen denotes many trials and defeats in life if it is found anywhere in the name or birthdate. Sudden calamities or unforeseen events seem to follow this number, and possible manifestations of the energy include illicit love affairs or money losses. Sixteen individuals will "crucify themselves on the cross of love," but can come into spiritual consciousness if they turn their love toward the "path of Light."

DUTY
4327
16

If Sixteen is found within the Soul Number, it may denote fallen ideals. If it is within the Destiny Number, it may indicate a "fall" through romantic love, scandal, humiliation, or marriage disappointments. If found in the Personality Number, it warns against misplaced affections. Sixteen people must learn to be faithful, to stick closely to duty, to be true to promises, and to remember the saying, "Pride goeth before a fall."

When this number is transmuted to the higher octave vibration, it expresses itself as love of humanity and the desire to uplift others in the cause of harmony.

Number Sixteen individuals must not become over-confident, but must analyze every action carefully. Consider the discrimination of the 6 coupled with the aggressiveness of the 1 and take time when making important decisions. Think of the refinement of the 6 as watching over the desires of the 1 in order to excel and to have a more serene, number Seven type of life. When silence and meditation are used as ways of overcoming, "mystics" can develop under this number.

The Listening: With your heart and soul, and be faithful.

Nineteen

Projects started some time ago are to be finished under this number. When the goal has been attained, number Nineteen individuals will feel an urge to start working with groups, pooling their energies with those of others instead of working alone.

TRUE
2935
19

Number Nineteens must use their gifts of compassion for the uplifting of all. This will test the true fidelity of the lifestyles they have chosen.

> "And Jesus said unto him: No man having put his hand to the plow, and looking back is fit for the Kingdom of God."
> Luke 9:62

To attain spirituality, these people must practice the Golden Rule, after which this number can express itself as a new golden cycle of opportunity.

> "I have set before you an open door."
> Revelations 3:8

The number Nineteen, however, has been termed a malefic. The person born under this number may undergo a "spiritual fall" through failing to live the life required of a truly spiritual individual, and by pretending one thing and living another.

> " . . . ye also outwardly appear righteous while within ye are full of hypocrisy and iniquity."
> Matthew 23:28

But when Nineteen individuals have determined to erase past mistakes, they may develop true spiritual character with unshakeable faith and a philosophy that will adequately sustain their resolves.

The Test: To work for self-mastery.

Chapter Nine

Through the Zero Octaves

As discussed earlier, the Zero represents God, Spirit, Divine Light, the All, the Absolute, unity, Creative Power. Rather than adding to or subtracting from the qualitites of another digit, it raises those qualities by a power. The Zero adds Divine protection; thus people whose numbers are expressed as a digit plus Zero show initiative and confidence.

Twenty

Those born under the number Twenty incarnate to be of service to souls who are ailing and in need of help. Such individuals give spiritual uplifting and guidance, and live the humanitarian ideal. Their keyword is "Universal Service." They have a call to duty. Their soul-selves know the danger of unbalanced decisions and realize that they must learn to toil carefully and bide their time in order to make wise choices.

By being aware of their inner soul life, they can direct their powers along positive channels and greatly benefit from their Cosmic gifts. Number Twenty people may feel a "call" to action in some great purpose, cause, or duty. Twenty stands for souls who have knowledge of both good and evil, and who must consciously exercise thoughtful choice to attain balance in all situations.

TOIL	TIME	WISE	BALANCE	DEATH	CROSS	WILL
2693	2945	5915	2131535	45128	39611	5933
20	20	20	20	20	20	20

This number contains the Zero, meaning that persons born under it are blessed with God's protection all along the way. Such individuals will toil patiently to overcome the conflicts of indecision, and they know within their soul-selves that they must seek inner guidance in order to accomplish their aims.

Twenty signifies "death" to a former way of life; a new outlook has been achieved through time and toil. Number Twenty people will bear the cross faithfully with the future crown in mind.

The Aim: The wise use of time.

Thirty

Our minds must continue to grow, to plan, to expand, and to manifest. Under the number Thirty, people can become confident and happy heralds of a new age of eternal life to come. As progressive and evolving beings, they face many circumstances as tests of their stability. They branch out in many directions, although sometimes unduly scattering their energies on projects of uncertainty. They feel the Zero power to go ahead, operating though trial and error. They are bound to go forward.

HAPPY	HERALD	ETERNAL	STILLNESS	GENIUS
81777	859134	5259513	129335511	755931
30	30	30	30	30

Thirty is a number of high endeavor. These individuals are aiming for fulfillment, and in the stillness of meditation they anticipate success through persistence and through faith in the help of God. They envision their future liberation from binding or limiting circumstances; inwardly they know that their own stamina will endure.

```
CHANNEL        MEDIATE
3815553        4549125
30             30
```

To pursue good habits which solidify into ideals of success is the purpose and goal of number Thirty people. By choosing right thoughts their lives become happy and joyful. Thus, they may become channels of blessings to many people, heralding constructive ideas, and they can serve their peers by acting as judges and mediators.

The Practice: Eternal benevolence.

Forty

Under the vibration of a number Forty we become ready to build our "city-four-square!" (Revelations 21:16) The city-four-square refers to a higher consciousness, one that is developed on all levels of living. Number Forty individuals know of the four levels of consciousness — reason, order, measurement, and justice — and understand that they must respond to the four spiritual laws — mental, emotional, physical, and spiritual — all laws of right and justice. They know of the "city not made with hands, eternal in the heavens" (II Corinthians 5:1) and understand that now they must be "squared away" in their actions and deportment. They must treat all with fairness and try to create universal harmony.

```
UNIVERSAL      HARMONY    POTENTIAL      AWAKENING
359459113      8194657    762552913      151255957
40             40         40             40
```

Often number Forty people must use their highest potential to maintain their forward-growing ideals and determinations. As in each of the incarnations under numbers that contain the Zero of protection, these individuals seem to have the imagination and ambition to climb each higher spiral of super-consciousness. The well-organized Forty aspirant always chooses to maintain an even keel of steadfast development.

The Emphasis: Patience and order.

Fifty

The purpose of this incarnation is to promote fusion between soul and body, which helps to unfold destiny leading to oneness. Life is a continuing education. The moment we stop learning we stop growing in that ideal consciousness keyed to Divinity. Working toward attaining transmutation is of primary importance for number Fifty individuals. They seek to learn real values relating to their ultimate goals, and obey the admonition to "Know Thyself."

```
TRANSMUTATION          KNOW THYSELF
2915143212965          2565 2871536
50                     50
```

Under the number Fifty, they may choose to explore the unknown and the exotic to satisfy the fantasies of their dream worlds. They believe that their rainbows of happiness will have the proverbial "pot-of-gold" waiting there for them. Their buoyant dispositions attract friends and good fortune, and they know how to take advantage of all these blessings — mentally, physically, and spiritually. They never let opportunities pass them by. Fifties create unique ideas and apply them to their work, thereby bringing success to daily efforts.

Number Fifty individuals await and are ready for a "Jubilee Celebration" wherever, whenever, and by whatever means the opportunity comes to them.

The Forecast: Release is to be accomplished.

Sixty

Through the life experiences gained in long cycles of evolution, the innate perfection of the number Sixty comes forth into manifestation. This individual is ever declaring, "It doth not yet appear what we shall be." (I John 3:2)

To "let go and let God" will help the gentle number Sixty person to hear the "inner voice" of guidance.

```
LET GO AND LET GOD        INNER VOICE
352 76 154 352 764        95559 46935
60                        60

COMMUNICATION             UNDERSTANDING
3644359312965             3545912154957
60                        60
```

The importance of communication between us and our Maker can prove to be one of the most valuable gifts of the Sixty vibration. It stimulates the Zero power in the hope of self-realization and understanding.

The mission of number Sixty individuals is to create harmony in their environment and to add to the beauty of this earthly garden.

One prominent characteristic of the Sixty is nurturing. These people want to take care of others, even beyond their immediate families. Their emotions run high, emblematic of the Cosmic Mother who nurtures all things. Because of their caring and devoted natures they are likely to be wonderful parents and loving mates. They can touch many hearts with messages of loving benevolence.

The number Sixty opens the door to the higher mind, letting loving energy flow outward toward those in need, helping them over the "rough spots" by supplying supportive good will and attention. Thus a love of all humanity is spread far and wide to awakening souls.

The Blueprint: Features benevolence.

Seventy

Number Seventy individuals are developing as potential channels for great truths of enlightenment; thus, they need lasting faith in order to continue expanding their mentality. The simple phrase "God is Love" was meant to create a spiritual bond for all humankind. Seventy people learn to give noble service patiently, not out of duty but because they want to serve others, and enjoy spreading the Light. "There is no mission so glorious as that of service to others."[1]

In the coming Aquarian Age, the hope of such an ideal is spread worldwide by means of radio, television, and the written word.

```
POTENTIAL CHANNEL   PATIENT PRACTICE     PROVE ALL THINGS
762552913 3815553   7129552 79132935     79645 133 289571
70                  70                   70
```

Good will is the desire to achieve harmony in right human relations because we know that the quality of each cell in our physical bodies is determined by the character of our thoughts. "As a man thinketh in his heart, so is he." (Proverbs 23:7) He that seeks, finds; and to him that knocks, the door shall be opened, for only by patient practice can one prove all things and enter the Temple of Understanding and Knowledge.

Growth occurs in cycles, as all living things respond to Cosmic Rhythm. For example, every seven years the body experiences a complete physical renewal. We are physical beings of thought, feeling, and action. Our etheric double is the link between the inner (soul) and our outer (physical) vehicles. We learn to conform to Cosmic Laws and Rhythms.

```
        EVOLVING ORACLE       LIFE LOVE LIGHT
        54634957 691335       3965 3645 39782
        70                    70
```

The laws of the Seven suggest that we are evolving oracles. Consider the cycles of human existence and how they relate to the number Seven.

1. Infant
2. Child
3. Adolescent
4. Adult
5. Power years
6. Wisdom years
7. Adept

The Seven bodies:

1. Causal
2. Atomic

3. Astral
4. The three-fold self
5. Intuitive
6. Mental
7. Spiritual

The Seven Laws of the Universe:

1. Fix the right goal
2. Good health
3. Education, preparation
4. Begin, drive
5. Resourcefulness
6. Perseverance
7. Guidance; God's help which is both first and last

The journey through time, space, and form is one of unfolding consciousness. In the Seventy, the cyclic progressions of Seven steps are enhanced by the greater dimension of the Zero power. Divine Energy is bringing each step of growth into prominence. The physical evolutionary cycles produce the Adept; the bodily cycles of growth produce the Spiritual Body, while the seventh law of the Universe brings the ultimate: endowing us all with God's guidance.

```
HE WALKED THE WATER
85 513254 285 51259
70
```

The Bridge: From the mundane to the spiritual.

Eighty

Through struggling with limitation we develop the power for enlightenment. Everything that Eighty individuals achieve is the direct result of their own thoughts. They rise, conquer, and attain through their own efforts. All that they have accomplished in other incarnations is now enhanced by the presence of the Zero power. Under the Eighty, we are helped by favorable vibrations to find our latent resources and attune them to greater heights.

Excellent achievements result from thoughts concentrated on the search for spiritual attainment and through understanding the importance of being dedicated to reaching for a further goal. Number Eighty people are under Divine inspiration to strive for, to reach, to achieve, and finally to attain that longed-for "Garden of Paradise."

```
SPIRITUAL ATTAINMENT     GARDEN OF PARADISE
179992313 1221954552     719455 66 71914915
80                       80
```

A growing consciousness is the purpose of human life. Material power and success are the fruits of living constantly with noble, lofty, and unselfish motives, with spiritual attainment as the goal. Positions of influence coupled with blessedness accrue to people who use their Eighty potential for the benefit of humanity.

```
GLORIOUS THOUGHT
73699631 2863782
80
```

Here is an example. A child born in the Arien Age (2,000-0 B.C.) became a great spiritual leader called The Buddha. Although he was brought up with every luxury, he renounced it all to try to discover the cause of world suffering. He vowed, at his great renunciation, to work to conquer world sorrow and disease. To discipline himself for that goal, he followed the "Noble Eight-Fold Path of Liberation," which teaches:

1. Right contemplation
2. Right mindfulness
3. Right effort
4. Right livelihood
5. Right conduct
6. Right speech
7. Right aspiration
8. Right views

Having attained his Illumination, the Buddha sent forth his disciples to preach to all humanity this doctrine of Divine Order that proclaims the perfecting of pure Godliness.

The Mission: To select the path of greater fulfillment.

Ninety

"In the beginning God created the heavens and the earth. And the earth was without form and void, and darkness was on the face of the deep. And God said, 'Let there be Light;' and there was light."
Genesis 1:1-3

The process of creation begins in darkness, formlessness, and chaos, but Divine emanation and glorious manifestation finally turn it again to Light. Although "in the beginning" all was darkness, Christian mysticism teaches that the purified mind transforms darkness to blazing light as humanity's vision spiritually unfolds within the seeking aspirant.

This symbolic theme is repeated yearly in the cycles of return. The winter solstice is said to be the deepest midnight of the year; the returning of greater light bursts forth in full brightness at every summer solstice.

```
FROM DARKNESS TO LIGHT
6964 41925511 26 39782
90
```

This can be seen as an episode of Divine Order and cyclic rhythm within nature which eternally teaches us of our own potential. Out of darkness the light emerges. The lesson is constantly repeated before our eyes for our realization. We "see" that the light of the soul reveals our true nature and that the light of intuition unfolds the nature of God in unity with humankind. Always held before us is the working of the Divine

Order. So it is here ordained that the self undergoes further awakenings and begins the work of regeneration in earnest.

The Triumph: Awakening to Spiritual Perfection.

Note

1. *The Golden Scripts* (Noblesville, IN: Soulcraft Chapels, 1951), chapter 49:71, p. 191.

Part Three

The Soul's Journey
through the
Master Numbers

Chapter Ten

Cycles of Becoming

One theme runs through all the messages of the double numbers, or Master Numbers, like a golden thread. Each is a variation on the one theme, which is the Eternal Truth: "I am here within thee — I the Living God."

"Lo, I am with you always, even to the end of the World."
Matthew 26:20

On this Earth plane, the plane of balance, we are faced with the positive and the negative, good and evil, the heights and the depths. We must make choices. Sometimes it is helpful to endure the depths in order to realize the heights. The conscious mind, which is the director of our lives, must weigh, balance, and reason in making the many choices that guide the responses we make to circumstances each day.

For example, a clergyman may be keyed to the master number 33 and thus, be expected to be something of a saint. The pressure of such a vibration will be a constant discipline, sometimes more than he can contend with. And his "flock" will be shocked if they find him exhibiting anything but the expected behavior.

In response, he may be subject to shades of depression and seek relief in various ways. Perhaps he is driven into various secret aberrations for relief. These diversions may take the form of sensual excesses. The flesh, with its five well-developed senses, seems to make demands for bodily responses.

Thus, he may live for a time under the digit Six — the underlying vibration of the master number 33 (3 + 3 = 6). The underlying Six of the 33 vibration is keyed to the social pleasures of human companionship. During such plateaus among the spiral risings, he may become attuned, temporarily, to the "pull of the world" and its temptations.

> "Liberation from the enslaving desires of the senses, and the reactions of the mortal mind is the aim and purpose of human life."[1]
>
>   Sai Baba

The conscious mind, which is the director of our lives, must weigh, balance, and reason in making the many choices that guide the responses we make to the circumstances we face each day.

$$11 - 22 - 33 - 44 - 55 - 66 - 77 - 88 - 99$$

These double digits represent vibrations of ever-increasing and ever-perfecting powers. Usually we are elated, excited, or dismayed when we find that we have master numbers in our Cosmic Patterns, and our first response might be, "How do I cope with them?" There are two possibilities: either we must strive to live up to them, or we may relax and live them as their digit sum indicates.

To live the life we envision as the master numbers come into cyclic rotation requires that we find means for purifying the body temple. (See Appendix C: Fasting.) "Know ye not that ye are the Temple of God, and that the Spirit of God dwelleth in you?" (I Corinthians 3:16)

We must supply our blood with the component parts of wholeness. Our blood is of great importance, for the health of the body determines the health of the soul. "The life of the flesh is in the blood." (Leviticus

17:11) Blood should be filled with the life force. "It is the blood that maketh attainment for the soul." (Ephesians 1:7) The red corpuscles in the blood attract oxygen through the fiery forces of the Sun and Earth. When our blood — and thus our brain cells — has its normal quota of iron, we enjoy a calm serenity of life and we are not upset by trifles.

In the process of blood purification, the "red" of Mars (Mars is related to iron) is to be transmuted to the "gold" of the Sun (gold is the metal of the Sun). The alchemists are said to have learned the secret of transmuting base metal (iron or lead) to gold, which should be interpreted symbolically as purifying desires of passion to the highest octaves of compassion. As we practice blood purification, the red (related to the element iron) is transmuted to the gold of the Sun.

The substance of "Being," sometimes called the Elixir of Life, is present in the blood. It is the material which works as a medium of purification and perfection in the brain. To accomplish this state of Being is to accomplish the Great Work. This is done cell by cell as we strive to become again the "Children of God." (Matthew 5:9) "If thine eye be single, thy whole body shall be full of Light." (Matthew 6:22)

> "On its way upwards on the ascending arc, evolution spiritualizes and etherealizes, ... thus the nature of everything that is evolving, returns to the condition it was in at the starting point — plus — a new and superior degree in the state of consciousness....Everything in the Universe progresses steadily, ... Nature is never stationary, it is always becoming, not simply being."[2]
>
> H.P. Blavatsky

The human body consists of a great colony of cells, perhaps as many as a trillion trillion. These cells form us and help us to be who we are. Cells have the power to reproduce, transform, and utilize energy, which is needed to promote breathing, moving, thinking, and blood circulating. We know that the cells have the power and energy needed for bodily functions, but they depend on being supplied with sufficient nutrients to maintain good health, well-being, and long life. All of the minerals and elements are necessary to the chemical make-up of each person who desires vigorous health.

> "Natural supplements are desirable, as synthetic products will not maintain perfect functions, as they act and react differently in the body. Therefore we must feed our cells well for the power within needs vital food, water, air . . . and . . . positive attitudes, as well."[3]
>
> Paavo Airola

We try to follow our mission, to come from the "water to Light," which means from emotional and passional consciousness to the compassional "Lighted Way."

> "When studied clairvoyantly . . . etheric blood is seen as a refined vibrating Light essence. The higher the attainment of the individual the more refined and luminous becomes the blood."[4]
>
> Corinne Heline

We know that matter is crystallized spirit, thus our part is to "metamorphose" spirit to "volatilized" matter. One of my teachers of metaphysics was said in an autopsy report to have had blood of a near amber color.

It is through the soul record, or memory, that we, in our travels from life to life, are able to improve and change the physical archetype and adapt it to conditions of the world. Eliminating the negative desires in the mind frees us of urges which bind and hold us to the confines of Earth. Unless the soul is maintained by prayer, meditation, and spiritual studies, the self cannot grow in heights of realization. But the soul knows that the same creative force which lures us to excess can, if reversed, raise the consciousness to illumination. The soul's potential must be activated by deep thought and understanding.

The Path, the spiral courses of humanity, progresses as we make our choices through faith and reason, as to "whom we shall serve, God or mammon."

"The consciousness of human beings is evolving and our point of focus is shifting upward to the heart center, which 'sits' midway between the three lower centers and the three upper centers. Human beings have shifted their consciousness upward from the solar plexus to the heart. Deeper aspects rest on a spiritual foundation."[5]

W. Brugh Joy

Cosmic Law tells of the soul's experience in the solar system. Humanity, in spiraling toward God-hood, has reached the Aquarian edge of attainment. Many cultural changes are affecting the collective consciousness of humanity, giving a glimpse of a potential civilization already unfolding before us.

The Akashic Records contain the soul's image and experiences. New thoughts bring new conditions by bringing out higher qualities into manifestation. No individual is better than or superior to another, as all have been endowed with the same degree of divinity. Degrees of development vary, giving some persons more insight and greater understanding, and an above average mental power to see, hear, and realize. Some are intuitive, clairvoyant, or clairaudient because of higher attainment in their past incarnations.

Such persons are undoubtedly incarnating under a master number, for the purpose of Earth evolution is to develop us into creators working in harmony with the Divine Plan. Spiritual unfoldment requires change. It is human to resist change, but no matter how good or how comfortable life may be, spirit will not let us rest there. It breaks up old conditions and old patterns of living, which are to be replaced by the Infinite Plan. Attaining spiritual consciousness requires continual dedication to something greater than ourselves. The goal is the attainment of that "mind that was in Christ Jesus." (Philippians 2:5)

Are we a finished product? No, we are far from finished, for anticipation and infinity lie ahead! We are here to become worthy of our origin, to develop character and the will to attain freedom.

Freedom — the power of choice — was the dangerous gift bestowed on humankind in the "garden." We are free to determine our own actions and reactions, to know good and evil, truth and falsehood, and to discriminate between them. Before the power of choice was given, we were in a state of innocence, but after the gift of free will, we assumed full responsibility and our destiny depended wholly on ourselves.

The soul innately desires to rise. The urge for study and enlightenment continues into old age, in the assurance that work is a waste of time if the occupation is for material gain only. Every hour spent in the search for enlightenment brings new light and hope of glory. Not until the uproar of physical life has subsided can we hear the "still, small voice" of spirit and behold the vision of ecstasy. Our most ideal joy is found in service to others. We learn to do right because we *will*, not because we *must*. We are free to choose.

Our potential is shown by what we have already achieved. Seeing what we have been — and what we may become — gives us much hope, encouragement, and strength to progress. Human effort must become higher and nobler.

The qualities in the master numbers have been recognized and held as ideals to aim for. In the Aquarian Age these will be more glorified as we come to understand their true significance better.

The master numbers (or double numbers) are not reduced to their digits; they are meant to be lived at their own highest value.They show the quality of the "missions" of the Initiate, or Adept. Initiation is an achievement, an attainment of the soul, which will succeed in dominating the personality, and in manifesting its true nature.

Thus, these particular numbers endow humanity with specialized and almost infinite opportunities. Double numbers intensify the digits. For example, a number 1 becomes aware of double its power as a number 11; a number 22 represents twice what was available under the digit 2, and so on through all the master numbers.

Our improving conditions could develop some day an Earthly Paradise, where the Will of God can be done, "on Earth as it is in Heaven."

Has not the soul, the Being of your life, at some time received a shock of awesome consciousness in some calm stillness?

Notes

1. Sai Baba, *Voice of the Avatar* (Andhra Pradesh, India: Sri Sathya Sai Books and Publications, 1950).

2. H. P. Blavatsky, *The Secret Doctrine,* Vol. 1 (Wheaton, IL: Theosophical University Press, 1946), p. 278.

3. Paavo Airola, *How To Be Well* (Phoenix, AZ: Health Plus Publishing, 1974), p. 207.

4. Corinne Heline, *Cosmic Anatomy and the Bible* (Oceanside, CA: Rosicrucian Fellowship Press), p. 229.

5. W. Brugh Joy, *Joy's Way* (Los Angeles: J. P. Tarcher, Inc., 1979), p. 194.

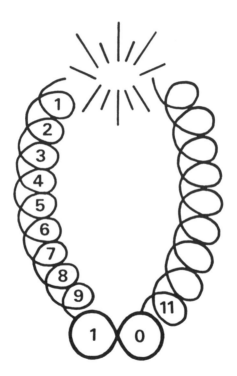

Chapter Eleven

Master Number Eleven

Master numbers accentuate the meanings of the single digits, and for that reason they are considered to be the most powerful vibrations. They symbolize the expansion of consciousness through a series of steps or illuminations as growth takes place, until the ultimate of Christ Consciousness is attained.

For example, people who have incarnated under the number 11 have not reached the heights, but they can draw on Cosmic aid for attainment. Their keyword is Altruism.

These individuals will be tested for their honesty and sincerity. They will be required to practice the "Golden Rule" and to live up to the standards expected of a master number person. The vibrations of number 11 are dynamic and extreme, and must be used with great wisdom. Number Elevens will naturally fall into leadership positions, and this requires the best humanitarian qualities they can muster. They will realize, eventually, that true mastership is service to others.

Pythagoras said, "Eleven is the number of a cycle of new beginnings."

When the forces of the Eleven become fully operative in people, they have the power to change their environments, to create new conditions, to build new bodies and new lives, all in harmony with the Divine Image in whose likeness they were fashioned in the beginning. Ministers, reformers, and charity workers come under this vibration, as do teachers, speakers, writers, promoters, and leaders in public service.

If these individuals use their master numbers to glorify themselves, however, they will experience loss and unhappiness. The Eleven is a very difficult vibration to handle; therefore, these people must be eternally watchful of their conduct. The rewards for fine performance are great, however, "the ends are well worth the means." The Great Work is the transmutation of matter into spirit. Then the spirit behind and within matter will be truly activated. Infinite consciousness remains constant wherever it manifests.

LIGHT
39782
29/11

Eleven combines the learner, number 1 (conscious mind) beside the number 1 of higher consciousness. These people think of themselves as individuals, as "1s" who have learned independence, leadership, and the qualities of aggressiveness necessary to cope with the world. Now, as 11s, or double 1s, they find the I AM beside them. Perhaps it is here that we learn of "I AM THAT I AM."

We begin to realize that in an 11 incarnation we will be tested as to how well we can make our lives express more oneness with our Creator. "God, as first cause, said, Let there be Light, and there was Light." (Genesis 1:3)

We should be inspired to "go, and do likewise," to try to create more Light in the world that we inhabit as physical beings. "The things I do, ye may do also." (John 14:12)

The qualities of unity and universality become manifest in developing 11 individuals. They can no longer remain apart, but must give of their Light to the world. An Eleven develops soul powers through graciously and lovingly giving selfless service wherever it is needed.

Eleven is the number of Light. It represents the hidden "knower." We live now in these spirals of awakening, where every philosophic thought should be considered, balanced, and judged for its value. We should not be biased by past beliefs or present appearances. We should have no favorite "isms" or theories. Truth must be the primary objective as we enter realms hitherto unknown or considered.

Through the power of seeing through appearances (visualization), we climb further on the "ladder of Light." We may use E.S.P. (Extra-Sensory Perception) as a method of seeing into the subconscious mind, but let us explore also our I.S.P. (Inner-Sensory Perception) as a way to examine the Divine Spark within us, which reveals the God-Power of the soul. Enlightened souls have unfolded a revelation of the spiritual potential and will strive the more toward total oneness, and eventually illumination.

We desire, more than anything in the world, to know ourselves. When old knowledge no longer serves our growth, or when we cling to it because we fear to leave it for the unknown, we are no longer growing. If some new revelations seem strange, we must develop patience and allow time for reflection. To attain perfection, we need to stay true to the higher laws of the numbers under which we are working.

The number 11 stands for the self and the Christ-Self, as a polarity within as One, though embodied in the flesh. A new birth has occurred in our hearts as a "seed" of immortality; we envision a brighter horizon. An inner voice calls us, as it called Abraham of old: "Arise, get thee out of thy country, into a land that I will show you." (Genesis 12:1) This new land meant a new and higher state of consciousness. "By faith, Abraham . . . when he was called obeyed and went out." (Hebrews 11:8) A growing faith brings realizations of what is meant by " . . . substance of things hoped for, the evidence of things unseen." (Hebrews 11:1)

When souls reach an 11 incarnation they are called "old souls." This expression is misleading. It does not refer to one old in years, or, older in terms of many incarnations, but older in reference to more growth in Light upon the Path. Such people are those who have glimpsed into what the Great Work will engender as they move toward the goal of Cosmic Consciousness. Jesus said, "Ye are the Light of the World." (Matthew 5:14)

Thus, we can derive that the Light Power within us demonstrates the power of God in Nature. "God is Light and in Him there is no darkness at all." (I John 1:5)

Individuals living under an 11 vibration must find the Light and share it with all who come within their realm, as these dawning states of consciousness work toward awareness of ever increasing order in humanity.

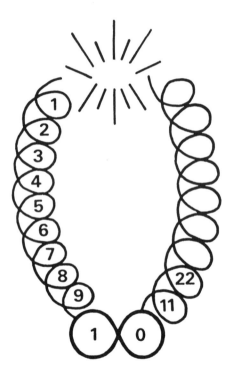

Chapter Twelve

Master Number
Twenty-Two

W e incarnate on a higher loop of the spiral under the master number 22. After having completed initiation as the 11 vibration, we are now here to apply our spiritual consciousness as best we can. The 22 vibration is more practical than the 11, so under this vibration we now determine to be spiritually helpful amid material world conditions.

Our knowledge as a master number 22 is gained during periods of quiet meditation and concentration. Thought energy increases as it is held at pin-point for later use as a dynamic power for worldly advancements.

A symbol that represents the understanding of the 22 is the "Tau," a letter of the Hebrew alphabet meaning the Cross. The Hebrew alphabet is called the "flame alphabet" because each letter is composed of little flame symbols, which are assembled in various combinations. These letters were held sacred and meaningful, as each one denotes a certain degree of illumination, leading towards the awakening of the Divine Love within. When the Great Work of the 22 master number is complete, the Cross becomes the Crown of achievement. The Tau Cross is not one of tragedy, pain, and defeat, but one of victory over limitation, indicating release into spheres of freedom from the bondage of matter.

PAIN
7195
22

Pain has its function. Pleasure and pain are closely related; it is our handling of these opposites that pushes us on to either success or failure. Each has a thousand faces and holds an equal number of temptations and tests.

"Pain that we cannot forget
Falls drop by drop upon the heart
Until in our despair
There comes wisdom
Through the awful Grace of God."
Aeschylus 525-426 B.C.

The awakening of Divine Love in us often comes through pain and loss. A crisis in life often leads us to turn to God; therefore, a crisis often comes before a more reverent and spiritual condition in life. Sometimes people can honestly say, "It is good for me that I have been afflicted that I might learn Thy statutes." (Psalms 119:71)

Pain is the quickest way of awakening us to a search for God. Pain without physical cause (mental or emotional pain) may be seen as a "seed" for a different life, a life of more purpose and deeper meaning. "Whom God loveth, He chasteneth." (Hebrews 12:6) Pain is a warning to do something, to use our excess energy more constructively. If we are emotionally or psychically hurt, we suffer intensely because of our high charge of unfinished evolution. We must find ways to let this pent-up energy pass. To eliminate pain we must achieve a new quality and intensity of awareness and express our energies in a new form of living.

"There lies before us, if we choose, continued progress, knowledge and wisdom."
Albert Einstein

Our real need is for an enlarged consciousness. Pain will disappear as evolution progresses. Truth reveals that love is finally ascended through pain, and not through pleasure. As pleasure marks the descension of the forces in the material world, so pain marks their ascension. Every ego makes the Prodigal Son journey through the Earth plane before being received into the Father's House, where the law of sin and death is superseded by the law of Christ's Love.

Selflessness is the key, the higher aspect of Vulcan, from which we are yet to receive our greatest benefit. This will symbolize a progressive way for those whose studies and practice have prepared them to follow the "Path of Light." Power to read the Akashic Records may also accrue here, but it must not be used for self-aggrandizement — there must be positive thought in this greater-will-energy. We came to Earth to learn how to control the Kundalini force, or creative power, and to create in the image of God through the spiritualization and perfected balance of the inner powers. Pain, anguish, grief, and despair challenge the soul to look beyond the plane of Earth life for happiness, beauty, joy, and peace.

WORK	GAIN	MIND	LORD
5692	7195	4954	3694
22	22	22	22

Number 22 individuals perform duty to many, no matter how tedious. They have the determination to finish whatever they start; thus, they bring to fruition many good works. This master number has the power of a double 2. It is positive in expression and contains the attributes of originality, diplomacy, and philanthropy. It calls for the use of intuition and organizing abilities if individuals intend to express the mastership of the number. If they are living less than their best, this number will express more as a 4 (2 + 2 = 4). Therefore, it is a challenge to be aware of what they can gain and expect from their cosmic gift of the wonderful master number 22.

Those born to demonstrate the master number 22 have to have patience, perseverance, and determination, and pay careful attention to details while maintaining a spiritual ideal within every organization uno'er their control. They are here to express high standards of honesty and courage while devoting attention to appraisal and value. The breadth of experience these people gained under the master number 11 has made them good teachers and they can serve as examples for others. The mission of number 22 individuals is to serve to the ultimate degree in material development and to direct others toward achievement in their own right.

People born under master number 22 cannot work for selfish purposes. They assume responsibility for the care and welfare of others while attending to work which may have been left undone by those who have failed. They always give more than they receive and expertly balance their lives in peace and harmony.

LILY
3937
22

The lily symbolically denotes the apex of glandular growth, finding its final development through the pineal and pituitary glands in the head. It also typifies the purity of the mortal aspect of the soul.

ROSES
96151
22

Red roses symbolize the downpouring of the planetary substances of the body's centers (or chakras) to co-mingle in the individual's heart center and thence into the blood. Thus, roses represent the compassion possible through the heart center, while the lily symbolizes the mind consciousness; yet the Lord presides over all combining the head and heart in wholeness.

Chapter Thirteen

Twenty-Nine/Eleven: Testing Number

W e climb the double spirals to again find ourselves in another life. But once again our number is Eleven. More is to be accomplished before we graduate to a higher plane. Our aim is high, but we must perfect each sense. We recognize the "I AM" as a focal point of energy; now we must increase and direct this energy rightly. Nothing is gained, however, without testing.

In its journey through the Earth plane, the soul meets trials and tests all along the way, and at some points may require an incarnation for more relaxed testing. Thus, interims of less rigid requirements are introduced between the high, double-digit incarnations. These interims, however, remain subject to the Eleven vibration, as the master number Eleven always influences the soul's behavior. This prevents a "cutting off" of the master rhythms which have been established. A reverence has been built within the soul for the higher cycles yet to come.

Three stages of experience lead to initiation: preparation, enlightenment, and initiation. The Eleven-type cycles are mostly keyed to preparation, for it takes a long time (a long series of incarnations on the Path) to attain all the knowledge of the higher worlds. A "testing number" properly used will reinforce devotion to the world of the soul's newly awakened memory of its original state in the heaven world.

The testing number 29 suggests an extreme: the vibration of the number 2 is in wide contrast to the number 9. This creates the possibility of having contrasting circumstances occurring simultaneously in the lives of individuals born under testing number 29. This forces them to choose wisely when making decisions about future conduct, with the help of many prayers and meditations. They should think of every problem as an opportunity to learn love and forgiveness, and to balance their lives as they work for harmony among all people.

CHOOSE	SPEECH
386615	175538
29/11	29/11

Only as we expand our horizons will we glimpse the glory of the oncoming Golden Age. Having attained this twenty-ninth degree of the testing incarnations, we work with determined effort that our progress will continue.

We chose the separation from God, so we must seek to return to God by our own free will. The coming Aquarian Age is a time when every soul will hear the voice within; a time when the Earth will be cleansed of its negative influences.

Speech is a sacred creative power. At the "fall" humanity lost communication with Divine Light. We were given the power of speech to use it wisely among our peers. It is important that we become conscious of our true selves. Self-mastery is our goal.

We learn correct breathing as a way to capture and hold more of the fiery energy. We seek to become "one" with all humanity. We enter our comrades' hearts, we speak with them patiently, we point out that their problems and woes are the same as ours, and that together we can grow. We enter their minds, we read their thoughts and learn to blend them perfectly with ours. Together we work for purity in thoughts and ideals. As we speak together, we "fuse" with their souls. We come to know them as they are and teach them to join with all of God's plan for peace and progress in the new age to come.

Work does not necessarily mean physical labor. Great strength can come through the use of mental powers, too. Employers and thinkers plan each day and work hard mentally to obtain their objectives; yet they may not do any physical labor. Physical and mental workers represent different periods of human evolution.

Faith in the power of mind enables us to progress from physical to mental works and to attract to ourselves whatever we wish: better financial conditions, an improved home environment, more satisfying relationships. Once we demonstrate our faith, the immutable Cosmic Laws become tools to help promote better decisions in our service to others. People of absolute faith know that, "As a man thinketh in his heart so is he." (Proverbs 23:7)

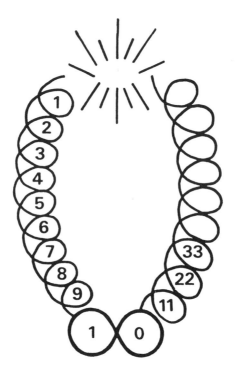

Chapter Fourteen

Master Number Thirty-Three

The mission of those born under master number 33 involves kindness and generosity. These individuals are as much concerned for the welfare of the world as for that of their neighbors. Plans for future improvements are envisioned, aimed for, and developed for the future good of all. Sacrifice and deep concern for others are part of the 33 incarnation; Christ-like ideals for healings and blessings are practiced. A blessing is an act of power, energy, and life, usually directed to someone's need. This may be done through the laying on of hands, or it may be sent by thought to the person in need. Giving a blessing is not just a religious saying; it is not just words. Things really take place while this master vibration is held in consciousness and used for the needs of others.

BLESSING	SAVIOUR	TEACHER
23511957	1149639	2513859
33	33	33

Neptune, the planet usually connected with spirituality, is associated with the master number 33, and is considered to be the higher octave of Venus. Expansion in consciousness due to the high Neptunian vibration is the mission of the master number 33 incarnation. Greater understanding of the inner worlds, perceived through E.S.P., reveals the reality of the afterlife. In the new Aquarian Age humanity will become aware, through the Light within, of the altruism and unity of this cycle, for the Saviour hath said, "I will never leave thee . . . or forsake thee." (Hebrews 13:5)

Those born under master number 33 are outgoing and giving of themselves in service to others. A keen sense of duty and justice underlies their conduct. They try to help reform those who indulge in negative or harmful actions. They attempt to answer the hunger for spiritual truth and make it satisfying to the masses. They strive to show this by setting an example of love and forgiveness in all their dealings. They minister selflessly to all who seek their aid. Their entire lives are spent in devoted service. Thus, they demonstrate their spirituality, not only as citizens of the Universe, but in many other planes of consciousness as well. "Other sheep I have which are not of this fold." (John 10:16)

The double number 33 is expressed as creative manifestation and expansion. This master number represents God's archetypal philosopher, reflected through the philanthropies given to others. We create every one of our conditions ourselves; we must watch our thoughts closely and cultivate the habit of cheerfulness in order to keep away from despair. We need to practice sending only kind and loving thoughts to others, in order to bring a harvest of glory multiplied manyfold. Wait in patience on the Lord for results. "Wait on the Lord: be of good courage, and he shall strengthen thine heart; wait, I say, on the Lord." (Psalm 27:14)

We cannot hurry a seed's sprouting-time-cycle, but we can eliminate old seed-thoughts by repentance and asking for forgiveness. Forgive yourself as well; never again let disgruntled thoughts "feed" on your soul substance. "We are transformed by the renewing of our minds." (Romans 12:2)

Control of the tongue also comes about by the renewing of the mind, the will, and by keeping a right desire in the heart. Live the sermon on the mount. Live the law of repentance. Live the law of obedience.

Blessed are they who endure temptation, for when they are tried, they will receive the crown of life which the Lord has promised to those who love Him. "Love God with heart, soul, and mind." (James 1:12)

Think love, speak love, give love, and live love! The master number 33 represents a very highly dedicated vibration. It indicates a "teacher of teachers" who is willing to sacrifice self for others, even to the point of becoming a martyr to an ideal.

Master number 33 individuals, on the way to regeneration, become teachers, speakers, or preachers, having wisdom and compassion for all. They no longer remain apart, but give of their Light to the world. When the Real Self controls their lives, and personal will is surrendered to the Higher Will, the birth chart no longer operates negatively. The astrology of the new age will teach this truth. This is the hope of the Aquarian Age. So, let this marvelous power within you take over and be you!

```
ALL IS WELL
133 91 5533
33
```

Chapter Fifteen

Thirty-Eight/Eleven: Testing Number

The prayer of individuals born under testing number 38/11 is to begin to see beyond the mundane and become aware of the valuable aspects and coming possibilities in spiritual growth and attainment. Their etheric vision will show them the way to break down barriers of race, creed, and color, and bring forth unity among all peoples as Light Energy permeates through all humanity.

We are now in the "edge of Aquarius," where vast new fields of wisdom are being opened up for our experiencing. Latent talent is emerging within individuals, and higher consciousness is increasing as our galaxy moves in space toward a more refined vibrational area in the Universe. Sound and color are being tested for their healing powers and for their application toward the well-being of all. Other wonders of experimentation begin to demonstrate the Oneness of all souls.

The process of evolution in consciousness must come from the mind, will, love, and understanding. Mental ability will become intellect as wisdom abides in God-human. A "new" human being is concealed in each of us. The higher level of teaching is all about our evolution, as we find in the Holy Bible and other sacred writings. In these books, the psychology of our potential is fully explained. It is likened to the idea that although we know that the oak tree is contained in the acorn, the acorn would wither and die without proper cultivation and nurturance. So is is with us. But cultivating our evolution involves not only food, light, and water, but also faith in a higher consciousness with extra-sensory powers.

Faith is the certainty of a higher level to be attained. Faith endows us with the knowledge that there is a higher and a lower, and that the lower obeys the higher. Thus, our senses obey a higher authority. If we say to our hands, "Write" and provide a proper instrument, they will obey. We must create ourselves, and not haphazardly, but by steadily and persistently working towards a goal.

Often people born with the number 38/11 will attain prophecy and clairvoyance through dreams or visions, which indicates that many of their spiritual awareness centers of consciousness are open to the "Greater Light."

PRAYER	FRIEND	FOLLOW ME
791759	699554	663365 45
38/11	38/11	38/11

Praying or chanting "AUM" stimulates the opening of these centers. After these centers have been opened, our faith never wavers. "Greater love hath no man than this ... that he will lay down his life for his friends." (John 15:14) This does not mean laying down the physical life of the body, but rather the willingness to sacrifice the "ego-self" to identify with the "I AM" consciousness. Thus, individuals with testing number 38/11 become of greater good to those who need them; their physical desires must be eliminated for the gaining of a greater good.

"Ye are my friends." (John 15:15) Friends are those who act beyond their own interests and live according to the sacred teachings of Christ.

"Whosoever shall save his life shall lose it, and whosoever shall lose his life for MY SAKE shall find it." (Mark 16:25) The keywords in this saying are *life* and *it*. "Life" as it is used here means the ego-self way of life, and "it" means superconsciousness. So we might say it thus: "Whosoever shall give up his selfish life shall gain superconsciousness." This is the challenge of the number 38/11: to surrender the ego for the ability to say, "Not my will, but Thine, be done." (Luke 22:42)

We are the seeds sewn on Earth as material for the Kingdom. It thus follows that humanity on Earth is an experiment in soul cultivation and evolution.

"Seek ye first the Kingdom of God and all things shall be added unto you." (Matthew 6:33) "Sell all you have and follow me." (Mark 10:21) To "sell all one has" means to rid oneself of false ideas, anxiety, and such; "follow me" means to choose the Divine way of life. To evolve to the "kingdom" we must first "sell" certain false standards; then we can buy whatever we value most, such as the "pearl of great price," which means the purity resulting from right choices in living.

These attainments are important as preparation for the coming incarnation on the master number 44 loop of the spiral path.

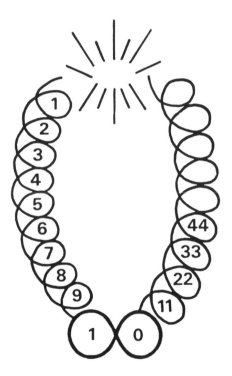

Chapter Sixteen

Master Number
Forty-Four

As spiritual entities, one with God, we are destined to grow, to develop, and ultimately to return to full communion with God. Nature is God in manifestation; we are God in the making. God's Will is not always done on Earth, but our will is expressed on Earth because we received God's gift of free will while in the "garden." Some may say, "There is no God" because horrible things happen on Earth; others may say, "If there is a higher Consciousness, why are we not told exactly what it is and what we have to do to reach it?"

```
SEED OF GOD
1554 66 764
44
```

We may not come to the new birth unless the "seed of faith" is planted and cultivated. If faith-truth falls on just a sense-based mind, it never takes root; it just withers and dies, but, "A little leaven will raise a whole loaf." (I Corinthians 5:6) This statement applies here, but the leavening experience must occur. It comes through a growing intensity of desire, insight, and conviction. Of course, difficulties arise, so achieving this level of consciousness takes time and patience.

Behavior must include forgiveness and practicing the Golden Rule at all times. Our ordinary will is raised to a more powerful will if the source of faith is opened within us.We realize we are working under a higher authority, and as this happens, our entire lives change, as do concepts of value. We ask ourselves: "What really is of value?" This kind of knowledge must be understood: we must realize that it is a change of will, and also a change of what we really love enough to "lose our lives" for. This is the type of living that prepares us for

```
ADEPTSHIP
145721897
44
```

The double 4 gives reason as the directing link to higher wisdom, and offers the potential for synthesizing the mundane and the spiritual for best results in action and leadership. Master number 44 individuals are resourceful and have complete strength and mental dominion over their activities. They understand financial values, but would work more toward the attainment of spiritual progress. The number 44 is a symbol that demands great self-control and discipline, one which brings with it a heavy burden and the possibility of becoming a world influence through conforming to the immutable laws of the Cosmic Order.

A growing consciousness is the purpose of human life, and the highest consciousness is the goal of human life. This growth goes forward and upward, spiral by spiral, from us as mere creatures to fully conscious Christed beings. Master number 44 people may attain this level of wholeness by controlled energy, thus enhancing their vitality and in turn activating the nerve centers in the brain. The creative energy retained within the body enables these people to attain mastery and to become illuminates. The Divine creative energy may be used either physically, mundanely, or for the highest creative ideal of Godliness.

Discipline is truly an act of love because it means that the seeker cares to achieve. Discipline takes time and patience, wisdom and devotion — all of these attributes constitute gifts of the spirit. This is a path each of us must take at some time in the on-going unfoldment of the soul. We are entering a period of extreme discipline, which can enhance our soul faculties and produce pure ideals regarding our relationship to God and how to become Christ-like.

"Now we are sons of God, it doth not yet appear what we shall be . . . but we know that when He shall appear, we shall be like Him." (I John 3:2) All of the Biblical Commandments, whether given by Moses on Mount Sinai or by Jesus on Mount Olive, are aspects of the One Law and reveal the means by which consciousness is disciplined in its unfoldment.

An old Chinese proverb says "When the student is ready, the teacher will appear." The teacher may be 10,000 miles away, sitting in meditation, and know nothing about the seeker personally; or, the seeker may know nothing about the teacher. Yet knowledge is received by tuning into the Omni-present Divine Consciousness.

Patanjali, a fourth-century Indian mystic, advises us that we would be helped by meditating on the heart of an illumined soul that is free from passion. When we are truly ready in our hearts and souls to know God and to receive God's Grace, to be free of our false appetites, jealousies, hates, and other selfish traits, when we are ready to be made spiritually whole, then the "teacher" will appear. Gratitude, love, and sharing are signs of a student's readiness. Selfish traits disappear and spiritual harmony is born. There is a "renewing of the mind." Spiritual discernment reveals the real Kingdom of God. Do not trust your five senses to reveal the Kingdom, but "judge with righteous judgment." (Acts 1:1-13)

We have been given etheric, or everlasting, bodies. These bodies provide us with the ability to transcend the material and respond more fully to the spiritual side of nature. This is the type of body we had in the beginning (before taking on the flesh body), and is the one we are all working to re-attain. We were first created in the etheric state and our memory is prodding us to return to that state. The memory consciousness is non-physical; it is a quality of the soul, of the I AM, of the Self. "Whoso eateth my flesh and drinketh my blood hath eternal life: and I will raise him up at the last day." (John 6:54)

FLESH BLOOD
63518 23664
44

Language conceals more than it reveals until we reduce words to their hidden meanings. All words are symbols. "In the beginning was the Word, and the Word was with God." (John 1:1) The written word is symbolic and will convey a message into the mind that will de-code it. The spoken word is a symbol bearing power, energy, and creative force, if God's vibration is within it. "I speak not of myself but of the Father that dwells in Me. He doeth the works." (John 14:10) "God said, Let there be Light, and there was Light." (Genesis 1:3)

The "Word" of God was manifest. Energy was projected into space by the Divine Creative Word, and there was Light. "The Word became flesh and dwelt among us." (John 1:14)

The Word is also used in healing. As the Word goes forth into the physical plane, healing takes place by the power of sound. Sound has force, behind which is the motive held in the mind of the speaker. Motive gives it life and feeling.

The seed of God, born into flesh and blood, grows to its God-hood, as good will, faith, love, and forgiveness are practiced in our lives here on the Earth plane.

Chapter Seventeen

Forty-Seven/Eleven: Testing Number

The soul's greater cycles consist of a series of Earthly incarnations with interim periods of testing during which pressure is lessened but still unremitting. The testing number 47/11 incarnation tempts the soul with the glamour of Earth's attractions; it appeals to physical desire and entices the senses. We can control our destiny by the way we think. We must be glad that we are being tried, because the trying of our faith helps us develop patience. "But every man is tried and tempted when he is drawn away by his own thoughts." (James 1:14)

Through testing, our brains grow sharper and clearer, and we learn discrimination. We must avoid idle thoughts, which are not productive or constructive for desirable growth toward wholeness. Doubt and fear are as weeds to a clear mind, and must be rooted out. Those who make no effort to control the mind will be left by the wayside of the Path of Light.

Original thinking and philosophical ideals will create a full harvest of hopes and progress toward our objectives. The practice of thought control is the most practical thing we can do, and the most worthwhile. Thinking is a planting and a cultivation of our desires to achieve mastership through love, health, and growth. It is not wise to linger in the past or to mentally wander through our memory banks. We really live in the present, and the future is the Lord's.

We have the incentive to seek and find reason to be glorified and blessed by way of demonstrating our faith in our future attainment and success. A rainbow aura may at times be observed around individuals who are truth seekers. If seen, it means that these people have desire for union with God and are striving for the attainment of brotherhood. "Man is a unit of that unity . . . his mission is to merge in the God from whence he emerged."[1]

```
INCENTIVE      SEEK AND FIND    MASTERSHIP
953552945      1552 154 6954    4112591897
47/11          47/11            47/11
```

Steadfast, disciplined meditation and training are needed to prepare the subconscious and superconscious minds to co-operate, but the effort can change us from mediocre persons into masters of concentration. Discipline is one of the most needed attributes in the greater cycles still ahead. The uniting of the subconscious and superconscious minds brings the most amazing results when accomplished; there comes a calm and peace almost beyond our understanding. Discordant and distressing thoughts no longer abound; only confidence and serenity pervade the mind.

```
MEDITATION
4549212965
47/11
```

Are we our brothers' keepers? More than we realize, for peace of mind cannot exist for us apart from our brothers and sisters. Unity of all people is the ideal of the Aquarian Age.

The soul underlies human thinking, feeling, and action. The body is an instrument of the soul, and we can observe that materialistic people behave one way, idealistic people in another way. Those who recognize themselves as souls, with their bodies as vehicles or instruments of the soul, will be inspired to search for truth. They will hope for salvation, visualize their own possible perfection, and yearn for immortality. The amazing energy which enables the great mystics to rise to freedom and dominate the world is latent in all of us.

"We are then, one and all, kindred of the mystics ... to participate here and now, in that real and eternal life, in the fullest deepest sense which is possible to man."[2]

Evelyn Underhill

Those who think of themselves as physical bodies only will lead a monotonous and mostly unprogressive life in terms of growth toward a higher consciousness. In the world-wide sense, this produces nations that fear other nations and thus take part in the ridiculous weapons race for supremacy. If humanity as a whole would accept the philosophies abiding in the master numbers, it would work toward a better civilization, one of tremendous possibilities in spiritual understanding and advancement for all.

The intense desire of the soul invokes the power for overcoming; other urges seem insignificant when soul desire is intent on attainment.

```
SELF CONQUEST
1536 36573512
47/11
```

We may still be tested for patience, endurance, and steadfastness as we wait upon the Lord.

"Wait on the Lord, be of good courage and he shall strengthen thine heart, wait, I say, on the Lord."

Psalms 27:14

"Truly my soul waiteth upon God, from Him cometh my salvation."

Psalms 62:11

People who incarnate under testing number 47/11 are faced with self-conquest with regard to the many enticements of the Earth plane. They must practice patience with those who seek to lure them from their chosen purpose. They must be above all steadfast in rejecting temptation, and must call upon their endurance to remain intact from illusions of the emotions. They are dealing with the combination of the number 4 (Earth) and the number 7 (Moon) working through the number 11 (Uranus). These three planets in aspect represent the gravity of the Earth. This pulls at the emotions (Moon), while the planet of surprises (Uranus) signifies possible unpredictable results. Testing number 47/11 people must have the courage to walk away and "wait on the Lord" for protection. "He that ruleth his Spirit . . . is mightier than he that taketh a whole city." (Proverbs 16:32)

The initiate Zoroaster, who founded the Persian religion, taught, "Keep pure your six powers, thoughts, speech, work, mind, memory and understanding."

ZOROASTER
869611259
47/11

Notes

1. Sai Baba, *Voice of the Avatar* (Andhra Pradesh, India: Sri Sathya Sai Books and Publications, 1950).

2. Evelyn Underhill, *Mysticism* (New York: E. P. Dutton & Co., Inc., 1955), p. 447.

Chapter Eighteen

Master Number
Fifty-Five

Each soul has a mission in the unfolding of its evolution, and it attracts to itself a time of incarnation, a name, a number, and a physical heritage in order to live out its purpose. Our planetary charts (or horoscopes) and the values of our birth numbers can show us exactly where we are in the space-time of the soul's incarnations in physical form.

Souls responding to the double number 55 are chosen to initiate new modes of life and thought on Earth. They have been learning to rule themselves with rigid discipline, and their will is quietly taking control.

The number 55 represents a fine creative spirit with keen insight that can help to balance difficult problems. People born under this number must believe in listening to those whom they serve so they can understand how to give them advice about attaining spiritual goals.

Looking forward to coming events can excite enthusiasm and inspire them to strive upwards along the Path of Light. Their touch into higher dimensions can stand as an inspiration for students of the number 55, for they have reached the point where they must try to light the way for all followers.

The underlying numbers in 55 (5 + 5 = 10 = 1) will be felt; therefore, they must be considered. The numbers 10 and 1 become helping

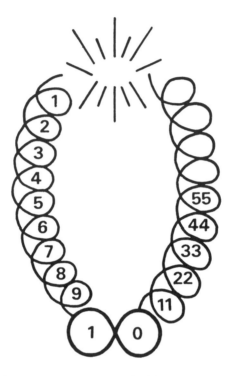

factors, having brought their own individual powers into the totality. (See earlier chapters for further descriptions of these numbers and their attributes.) We have learned that the 10 represented the "conversion point," and brought its own power for even greater cycles of attainment toward unity by making available qualities from the ten stages of mind unfoldment. The basic unit 1 calls for demonstration of the In-dwelling Presence, leading others toward the Path of Light.

The double five takes us to the verge of change in conscious functioning — possibly to a higher way, cosmic in scope and vast in possibilities. We have come a long way but the ultimate power of the mind is still ahead. The scientific approach to Christhood is useful, and a further plan is developing. A whole mind — the two hemispheres of the brain working in unison — is realized when thinking becomes infinite, unlimited, and spontaneous. A new understanding of ourselves and of the physical world becomes apparent.

```
THE MEDIATOR
285 45491269
55
```

Mediators work toward the blending of the many religious creeds, urging them to combine their efforts to bring about more unity among humankind. The ideal that religions may be replaced by true spiritual values is a goal of universal unity. The ideal of right relations between nations, as well as between individuals, should come into focus when each unit of humanity thinks not as a member of a particular race or nationality, but as a planetary citizen of the Universe. Master number 55 people realize that it is necessary to visualize future accomplishments for the benefit of all people on Earth, not just for their own race or nation. "For there Is one God and one mediator between God and man, the Man, Christ Jesus." (I Timothy 2:5)

The idea of the United Nations is a very old dream, but it is a "seed" for a vision for us all: that nations should evolve, integrate, and cooperate as one. What an ideal way to solve world problems! As interdependence becomes more urgent, our leaders will see that cooperation is the only answer, the only way of healing the differences among us. Nations must learn not to fear other nations; then disarmament can take place and the resources of all countries can be shared among all people.

From new patterns of thought under the master number 55 will come the ability for mental telepathy, healing, astral projection, clairvoyance and prophecy, as well as other developments of ever increasing order. Sociologically, we will see all others as aspects of ourselves; thus, fighting with one another will cease and peace on Earth will prevail. Mind, the builder, works hand-in-hand with the will to accomplish greater goals in consciousness. We are concerned with the problem of freeing our souls from the Earth's gravity. All developed seekers are aware of this truth.

"The liberating truth is that physical forces, and all other forces, are essentially spiritual because their root is the Divine Life behind all things."[1]

Paul Foster Case

```
WILL TO EVOLVE
5933 26 546345
55
```

As the Piscean Age draws to a close, the mission of master number 55 people will come into the consciousness of certain other developed individuals who will act as catalysts for further growth. The change indicated has not been attainable in its full Cosmic intent as yet, but will become noticeable as the Aquarian Age consciousness begins to be felt. The true soul consciousness is aware of the spirit within and its identity with God, and now may express this knowing of all it has experienced.

The free will now chooses meditation and prayer as a way to the spiritual, as a definite direction God-ward. By Divine Inspiration, urges to fulfill the mission of the master number 55 in the present life become of major importance. No matter what the past has been, the future is within our power of choice to work toward our chosen goals. From this point on, the admonition "Choose ye this day whom thou shalt serve." (Joshua 24:15) becomes the watchword. Thus, the soul may become like a shining star in the Cosmos.

Humanity, from the time of Pythagoras and Plato, has discovered helps along the way of evolution and has left its legacies for us to use. Around 600 B.C., Lao Tzu wrote a book called the *Tao Teh King*. Tao means "streams of consciousness" (the way of life); Teh means the "unfolding of life." Taoism, a religion of China, is devoted to the belief of humankind's mystical union with the Ultimate. The sacred writings of all ages show the same Ultimate Divine Pattern.

The mediator proposes and strives to promote a way of life between the Omniscient God and the developing self. This sums up the progression of the master number 55 aspirant who is climbing the ascending spirals of higher consciousness.

Note

1. Paul Foster Case, *The True and Invisible Rosicrucian Order* (York Beach, ME: Samuel Weiser, Inc., 1985), p. 176.

Chapter Nineteen

Fifty-Six/Eleven & Sixty-Five/Eleven: Testing Numbers

In numerical sequence, two phases of the number 11 lie between the Greater Cycles of Divine Order (the doubles 55 and 66) and must be delineated. These are the 56/11 and 65/11 cycles. Let us first review the appropriate symbology.

1. The number 5 represents mental powers, the reasoning mind, judgment, and change of outlook; it is linked to the planet Mercury. It is natural for us to intuit a higher potential and search for greater soul attainment.

2. The number 6 represents emotion, love, desire, glamour, beauty, and the urge for ease and luxury; it is associated with the planet Venus. Love that is beyond the level of the personal or the sensual takes us into other dimensions, where love of all humanity reigns in consciousness.

3. The number 11 stands for mastership, the higher mind, super-conscious-steps-of-unfoldment, and balance; it is connected with the planet Uranus. In the heightening of consciousness, there is a development of a further kind of intelligence: wisdom.

The quest is for the expansion of consciousness. Each incarnation is like a day at school. Clues about the level of development of consciousness are revealed through the value of the numbers in the individual's name and birthdate. (Further clues can be found in the planetary chart.)

To read the symbology of the double numbers, we work from right to left. Thus, in the testing number 56/11, Venus (6) is vibrating through Mercury (5) for the 11 effect; in other words, love (Venus) working through reason (Mercury) for a better balance. "As a man thinketh in his heart, so is he." (Proverbs 23:7)

MANIFESTATION	PROGRESSION
4159651212965	79679511965
56/11	65/11

In the testing number 65/11, Mercury (5) is working through Venus (6), which means that the mind's reasoning power vibrates through the emotions, or love consciousness, to attain greater understanding and unity. These attributes within us — head (reason) and heart (love) — must combine to allow the "mind to love, and the heart to reason."

Once individuals have attained an 11 incarnation, it is rare for them ever to drop back below it. They may reach a plateau between the greater cycles, but may still express another of the many phases of the 11. Individuals cannot rise into higher initiations until the former ones are firmly set. They work in the interim incarnations until the time is ripe for the next growth period. When they are ready, their souls accept the assignment and determine to cope with the next challenge.

The perfect law of manifestation should be used to produce joy, abundance, health, and vitality. Blessings from God come from obedience to the law. To work for the purpose of regeneration, the seeker needs to awaken Divine sensitivity in order to analyze concepts intuitively. The soul within comes into direct contact with the Over-soul, or super-consciousness, to help bring the things this individual hopes for into manifestation.

In the order of spiritual evolution within our Solar System, the soul passes through many states of consciousness in its growth toward Oneness with God. We all undergo the process of birth and development, demonstration of ability, and transition, after which a renewal of vitality in the non-physical realm leads to physical re-birth.

```
CHRISTHOOD        ENLIGHTENMENT
3899128664        5539782554552
56/11             65/11
```

The attainments of all the 11s increase as the cycles are repeated over and over in consecutive life-wave-refinements throughout eternity. Memory is retained in the cells, and is responsive to stimulus, thus constantly initiating action and re-action. Physical and mental development seem quite complete, but emotional and spiritual development are far from finished. In the degree we seek Divine guidance, we may proportionally benefit from God's plan for us. Former abilities may be restored, new levels of skill and talent may be developed during the successive cycles.

> "Eye hath not seen, nor ear heard, neither hath entered the heart of man, the things which God hath prepared for those that love Him."
>
> I Corinthians 2:9

In these cycles of growth we may expect greater advancement in philosophy, creative art, and science. As we enter further into areas of consciousness, each key unfolds its message and mission.

```
TO WALK THE WATER
26 5132 285 51259
56/11
```

As the wisdom in each rising spiral adds bit by bit to the fabric of the soul's totality, the Master Motivator within us inspires us to build our Temple of Light as a daily work and privilege. We realize that we have within us the potential for building the ideal vision of the twelve-pointed star, or the diamond body of brilliance. This had formerly seemed like an impossible dream, but the wonder of uniting the head and heart in consciousness could create the harmony of complete happiness called bliss.

MASTER MOTIVATOR
411259 462941269
65/11

We are now beginning to understand that a human being has both material and spiritual powers and abilities latent within the total being. These powers are not miraculous, but simply expansions taking place in the greater cycles of Divine Order, although at this time these talents mostly appear among enlightened individuals of the higher cycles.

RECAPITULATION
95317923312965
65/11

As head and heart cooperate fully, progress can accrue toward adeptship. We seek to be in readiness for the challenging master number 66 cycle and anticipate the work of a coming incarnation.

Chapter Twenty

Master Number Sixty-Six

The Aquarian herald is one who meditates on love and is travelling the path that leads to the Temple of Initiation. Consider the equation 66/12/3 (6 + 6 = 12 = 3). Between the 66 and the 3 is the 12 vibration, a greater cycle in symbology. (See chapter 8, Special Numbers.) As we have learned, numbers underlying the double digit master cycles exert influence, either positively or negatively. As 12 is not a master number, at times the point of view of mass consciousness could constitute a reversal of constructive vibrations to those of lesser values, or a conflict between the two. People born under master number 66 know that their continued growth depends on the obedience to Cosmic Law; thus, they retreat into meditation for re-centering. The self-sacrificing Vulcan (2) working through the aggressive ego of Mars (1) presents the problem, at which time the resulting number 3 (Jupiter) beneath the number 12 must bring about a return to ideals of benevolence and service to others until the greater cycle 66 is re-established and stabilized.

The number 6 relates to love and passion; the master number 66 relates to love as compassion, offers a philosophy of Divine fulfillment on Earth, and defines humanity's spiritual laws which are hidden in the hearts of us all. God needs humanity; it is Love calling to love. Love

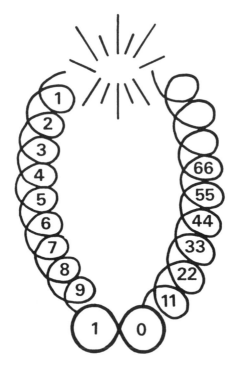

and forgiveness came with the Piscean Age, just as unity of all peoples and compassion will pervade during the Aquarian Age. The law of the Piscean Age was, "Love ye one another even as I have loved you." (John 15:12)

```
AQUARIAN  HERALD        SPIRITUALIZE
17319915  859134        179992313985
66                      66
```

In the future, we can expect holistic humans to live their soul qualities. Initiates of the 66th degree have attained much toward God-hood. They are the philosophers who work through understanding of all things of the soul and know that happiness depends upon it. Compassionate love must be learned and expressed on Earth while we are in physical bodies. All human beings are Gods in the making; thus, the awakening of the God within is as the return of the Divine in our hearts and minds.

NATURAL PEACEMAKER
5123913 7513541259
66

When passion is raised to compassion, we have learned the lesson of the master number 66, and we stand as a friend to all in the shadow of God. We have worked to develop a direct link with Universal Consciousness and Divine Wisdom. In the 66 level of consciousness, human desires such as lust, greed, hate, envy, and all other attributes of the lower senses must become fully subject to the Christ within as the plane of love relates truly to the plane of thought. The transmutation of love (passion) to agape (compassion) is often gained through the working of opposites: pleasure and pain, or joy and sorrow. Deep emotional experiences gradually build strength into the soul.

Sometimes even a broken heart must be endured, for a broken heart is one that is open to instruction. People who have had no sorrow that has made them turn to God are the ones to be pitied. Tears may be necessary until we learn obedience without bitterness. "The Lord is nigh unto them of broken heart, and saveth such as be of contrite spirit." (Psalm 34:18)

The soul is always closest to God when undergoing deep agony and longing. The substance of one's soul may need to be watered with tears to make it productive of the greatest blessings. Often the most poignant sorrow leads to the greatest achievement.

> "We build our fortunes thought by thought
> For good or ill, yet know it not.
> Choose then thy destiny and wait,
> For love brings love, and hate brings hate."
> Ella Wheeler Wilcox

Cosmic Consciousness can be described as an awareness within each soul, imprinted on the mind and waiting to be awakened by the Will of the soul's oneness with God. After we have learned obedience to God's laws, there is no longer any need for suffering to find God.

KINGDOM OF GOD
2957464 66 764
66

Personal transformation was the original American dream. A new spiritual age is dawning; our new lives will be aimed toward cooperation, and goodwill, expressing unity with all beings and restoring peace to the world.

AN AMERICAN DREAM
15 14599315 49514
66

Symbology in Raphael's Paintings

In the painting *The Sistine Madonna* the Pope is represented as pointing to the Madonna and the Christ Child. A close examination of the hand wherewith he points will show that it has 6 fingers. There is no historical evidence to show that the Pontiff actually had such a hand, neither can the fact be an accident. Therefore it was put there by the design of the painter.

In the painting *Marriage of the Virgin* a similar sign can be seen. Mary and Joseph are shown together with the Christ Child, as though on the eve of their departure for Egypt. A Rabbi is in the act of joining them in marriage. The bare left foot of Joseph is in the foreground of the picture. You will notice that it has 6 toes.

By these symbols Raphael intended to show that both the Pope and Joseph possessed a sixth sense such as is awakened in the forerunners of the new type of Aquarian.

THE LIGHTED WAY
285 3978254 517
66

Tradition has recounted that the Atlantean Mystery Temple was a school of soul growth, revealing the Path of Love as the mission of the adept of the new age. This is the path of the heart, tenderized by the practice of total love and compassion towards all, "Earth love must grow into Heaven Love, heaven love must grow into Earth love, and mix . . . and be one twain."

```
LORD     JESUS     SAVIOUR
3694     15131     1149639
22       11        33      = 66
```

This is the law of the Cosmic transmutation of Kundalini, which cannot come until the seeker has worked for it and learned it. Remember, in creating the "Philosopher's Stone," go slowly and carefully and always by way of the heart. It is God's most holy dream that all people create and obtain the "Philosopher's Stone" and the "Elixir of Life" (veiled names for the birth of the Christ within).

```
FAITH IN ACTION
61928 95 132965
66
```

If you bear the cross, bear the pain of crucifixion, bear the tests of faith, the loss, the emptiness, the aloneness — then will come the resurrection and glory. This is sometimes called the "death of the lesser self." Waiting, darkness, sadness, and silence always precede joy, love, dawn, and fulfillment. We cannot have our "ascension" without the crucifixion. God-awareness is awakening more and more as we approach the new age of Cosmic Love.

> "The measure of any man's progress toward his own omnipotence is gauged by the measure in which God-consciousness is awakening in him."[1]
>
> Lao Russell

Note

1. Lao Russell, *Why You Cannot Die* (Waynesboro, VA: University of Science and Philosophy, 1972), p. 17.

Chapter Twenty-One

Seventy-Four:
Testing Number

*Approach ye genuine philosophic few, the Pythagoric Life be-
longs to you.*

Thomas Taylor

T he problem in this interim incarnation is to keep away from fantasy.
Those born under this number must determine from what plane they
are being tested. They ask themselves, "What is the danger this time?"

Let us analyze the numbers being faced here, reading from right
to left. The number 4, representing Earth's conditions and attractions,
will be working through the number 7, the Moon's domain of emotions
and fascinations, to try to bring about the Super-consciousness of 11
(Uranus). This is a tremendously difficult requirement.

```
COSMIC FASCINATION
361493 61139512965
74/11
```

When the materialistic Earth consciousness exerts its pressure on the
Moon's emotional consciousness, individuals must diligently watch the
events that come into focus. It will be difficult to cope with lower and
more Earthly limitations after having (hopefully) attained the heights

of the 66th degree. The Moon increases creative imagination; thus, it may be expressed as an attraction leading testing number 74 people away from the strictness of the higher path. Under its influence, they may build "castles in the air," which could lure them far afield from their original intentions. They may lose, thereby, some of what they have gained in some of the former incarnations.

When they have made a thorough examination of the dangers involved, they will quickly intuit what they need to avoid among the ever-present alluring temptations of the Earth plane. When this is done, the path will be straight, but not easy. The best procedure, if followed, will prove that the "end is well worth the means." The "end" is seen as that glorious glimpse of Eternity, or the Kingdom of Heaven, that is shown as a possible attainment once we have stilled our minds in deep meditation upon the cyclic order. The practice of listening for the "still, small voice" is one way of attainment, a way in which the "speech" of the stars or the "music of the spheres" (which is audible to the interior hearing of the initiate) may be heard. (This was taught by the Pythagorean school).

```
NEO-PYTHAGOREAN     INFINITE JUSTICE
556 77281769515     95695925 1312935
74/11               74/11
```

One must be both aggressive and receptive to handle the Universal Forces wisely. Limitations, sorrows, and pain tenderize us and lead us to search for answers. We learn that when we change ourselves, our environment also changes. As groups of people "catch" the ideal, humanity will slowly progress toward the inherent Divinity planted within us at the beginning. The soul knows that the same creative energy which lures us to excess, can, if reversed, raise our consciousness to illumination.

The Cosmos is striving to bring forth divinity-inspired-self-conscious-awareness. This is possible within the evolution of the human kingdom. Involution is nature working down through the elements; evolution works up through the principles of justice within Divine Law.

```
CRADLE OF LIBERTY
391435 66 3925927
74/11
```

Many of our ancestors have been willing to lay down their lives for their countries. In the United States, the founding patriots called their new nation the "Cradle of Liberty." Much progress has taken place throughout the years because of the freedom won by our early pioneers. They had faith and confidence in the future peace and harmony in the new land.

Faith is as a living, active seed, not merely passive belief. This seed must be cultivated in order to grow. We must express confidence and act as though the belief is unshakable. If we have faith as a "grain of mustard seed" nothing shall be impossible to us. Even the smallest seed of faith will grow within if confidence of its power is allowed to expand; this will tap the level of mind above ordinary visible things. Faith is not of the body, it is of the soul. Daily practice of faith can fulfill a longing for something beyond everyday living: the spiritual longing for Cosmic Consciousness. All sacred teachings come through faith and a certain kind of love, through the intuition of one who listens to the "still, small voice."

```
TEMPLE OF THOUGHT
254735 66 2863782
74/11
```

Materialistic individuals do not live at their highest level. They must be disciplined in this process. Be aware that negative thought can sprout and grow quickly, like weeds, and if allowed to run on may destroy a crop of hope. We all may move out of such undeveloped thinking and enter into the new spirals of thought yet to be established. The human race is not yet complete. A new level awaits us, and only we can complete ourselves.

We must not take it for granted that the soul is already "there" in consciousness, but must recognize that it has the potential for attaining Super-consciousness. Although our souls were created in perfection, they now express the result of what we have made them with our own free will.

We are at the threshold of the transformation of consciousness. As we progress on the Path of Return, we will come to a place where it is necessary to sacrifice the worldly in order to reach the spiritual. This step of the spiral is approaching the

```
BRINK OF A MIRACLE
29952 66 1 4991335
74/11
```

Note

1. Thomas Taylor, *The Theoretical Arithmetic of the Pythagoreans* (New York: Samuel Weiser, Inc., 1975), p. v.

Chapter Twenty-Two

Master Number Seventy-Seven

In the master number 77 level of consciousness we become aware that we are spirits and that we must reflect and meditate on past progress to gain new perfection.

Am I my "brother's keeper"? The realization comes here and now that peace of mind does not exist for any one of us apart from our brothers and sisters. The unity of all peoples is the ideal of the new Aquarian Age. People will see with greater wisdom, which will break down barriers of race and creed, and bring forth this Aquarian consciousness.

```
AWAKENING AQUARIAN
151255957 18319915
77
```

The soul evolves through love. The essence of a soul is always a part of the Cosmic Soul, which manifests in countless expressions. Each of these expressions occurs in another personality. The soul cannot be lost because the essence of all the personalities blends into the complete Cosmic Soul, just as the colors of the spectrum blend into a pure white light.

The soul does not lose its personality during the change called death. Our Lord Christ is still the Living Christ, although He, as Jesus, passed through the bodily change called death. The Christ manifested a body that was built under the powers represented in the master numbers. In the interval between the resurrection and the ascension, He appeared to His disciples, telling them to view Him in His garment of Light, "Behold my hands and feet, that it is I, Myself, handle Me and see." (Luke 24:39)

The Christ here describes the regenerated body which is immune to disease, age, and even death. This is the immortal vehicle He taught others to build. He said, "I am the way, the things that I do thou shalt do, and greater things." (John 14:12)

When one of the disciples asked Him, "How shall we know the way?" Jesus answered, "I am the way, the truth, and the life, no man cometh unto the Father but by Me." (John 14:6)

The word "Me" contains a hidden symbol. Watch the many times Christ in His teachings uses this word. In ancient Kabalah, "Me" numerically stands for Christ consciousness.

$$M = 8 \text{ and } E = 5 \text{ thus } 8 + 5 = 13$$

The number 13 stands for transmutation — raising the kundalini force. It is the kundalini force that brings illumination or Christ-consciousness. (This sample is given to show the way the ancient writers of the Bible used "code" and symbolism to explain their meanings to the "inner schools.") Following are some quotations where Jesus used the word "Me."

"Let not your heart be troubled, ye believe in God, believe also in Me."

John 14:1

" ... the Father in Me, he doeth the works."

John 14:10

From the law of the 11 we learned to use our power to spring upward into our rightful new vision, new health, and new view of life. The 77th

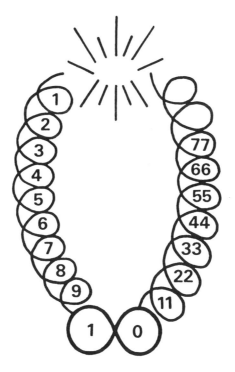

state is like a temple in character, with mystical powers in action. With character comes judgment, and in this cycle we become known for our wise counsel.

```
THE  TREE  OF  LIGHT
285 2955 66 39782
77
```

The Tree of Light has many branches, (physically the nervous system and blood bodies). Enlightenment spreads in all directions. During a master number 77 incarnation, individuals seek to purify the mind, body, heart, and action. If they are builders, they strive to create better structures; if they are scientists, they seek to discover new ways to help humanity; and if they are teachers or preachers, to present the wisdom and love that engender peace. As healers or philosophers, they inspire visions of hope and grace.

CYCLES TOWARD ONENESS
373351 265194 6555511
77

Here we begin to deal with mastership and mysticism. Mysticism is right thinking with our vision God-ward where we live anew. Those born under the mystic master number 77 develop in the practice of silence, aloof and alone. They are workers in the Cosmos, and their tools are the latent forces of Divinity within all life. The lonely way is also the Lighted Way. Be not afraid of loneliness. The soul who cannot stand alone has nothing to give. Loneliness is one of the first things that indicates to disciples that they are being prepared for initiation. Disciples stand detached and unafraid in that place of utter quiet when the Master comes. Individuals who learn to live as souls set pure examples of spiritual living. They must be able to endure aloneness to enter the spiritual life. Sometimes aloneness is the price we pay for the spiritual. We may be misunderstood or persecuted while climbing the spiral of the master number 77 incarnation.

We need to attain "holy emptiness" from all past mistakes, by practicing faith in God. The heart must be without greed or resentment, after which it can be filled with love and forgiveness for all humanity. We must turn away from the masses and toward God, and develop a love of being in God's company. Then we realize we are not alone; we have a "presence," a power within us; we have tasted the mystical experience, sometimes called the "Mystical Marriage," a conscious union with God.

Consider the equation: 77/14/5. The underlying numbers 14 and 5 subtly influence the master number 77. Number 14 individuals have wayward dispositions which, in the higher vibration, sometimes shows as fixity of purpose. The physical malefic 14 still leans somewhat to the sensational, but usually the 5, with its ability to make fair adjustments, is a foundation for the needed change of intent. To keep the danger under control, master number 77 people need to be aware of the possible rebellion in the underlying nature of this number. They must be ever watchful.

```
ELECTRIC  ENERGY
53532993  555977
77
```

All our energy is electrical in essence.

" . . . electricity is an entity . . . electrifies into life and separates primordial matter into atoms, themselves the source of all life and consciousness."[1]

H. P. Blavatsky

The mystical Path is the most difficult and subtle path to tread. Divine knowledge is not taught in words, but by recognition of knowing from within. We may be outwardly awake, but inwardly asleep. It is when we begin to "stir in our sleep" that awakening is possible. "Awake, O Sleeper, and arise from the dead and Christ shall give you Light." (Ephesians 5:14)

The soul has a purpose. It seeks any incarnation that will be constructive toward its growth. Just as an acorn has the intention of becoming an oak, so the soul's intention is to become God-like. Somewhere in its journey from life to life, a flash of enlightenment comes, as it constantly pursues its destiny. On this journey, the soul meets many obstacles and tests. We may choose to use every problem and sorrow as opportunities for solving and learning, by analyzing conditions for causes and searching for ways of understanding. Methods for overcoming will be revealed to us as we develop our expertise within the greater cycles of growth.

We have the keys to dynamic power in our hands when we refuse to be victims of self-pity. If one truly has faith, one has power. All things must produce after their own kind. Thoughts are as seeds carrying energy toward growth; thus, what the mind dwells upon must come forth, must manifest.

```
SPIRITUAL  ORDER
179992313  69459
77
```

The Universe is ordered from the atom to the stars. The Universal Intelligence penetrates everything seen or unseen. As consciousness expands, greater concepts must follow. Material science made great leaps in the Piscean Age; the spiritualization of the science of the soul is expected in the Aquarian Age of brotherhood and altruism, as we pass from physics to metaphysics, chemistry to alchemistry, and psychology to parapsychology.

Note

1. H. P. Blavatsky, *The Secret Doctrine,* Vol. I (Wheaton, IL: Theosophical University Press, 1946), p. 142.

Chapter Twenty-Three

Eighty-Three/Eleven: Testing Number

This number indicates that it is time to be in Divine Order and develop strength in all areas, physical, mental, emotional and spiritual. Jupiter (3), which is expansive and idealistic, is influencing the powerful and conservative Saturn (8) to bring forth unlimited growth in consciousness, Uranus (11).

```
IN DIVINE ORDER     THE SHIELD OF FAITH
95 494955 69459     285 189534 66 61928
83/11               83/11
```

The challenges of the testing number 83 will be those of concern that, while climbing the spiral toward Divinity, material opportunities might distract the soul from its true purpose of returning to God. The Lord Christ teaches us that while we live in our physical bodies, we are to keep them refined and pure so that we may make our "Temples" fit dwelling places for the God within. Christ's teachings describe a process of refinement to the point of immortality.

We want to attain wholeness, to unite body, soul, and spirit in complete harmony. We heighten and brighten our lives as we determine to regenerate the body.

"Consider the lilies how they grow; they toil not, they spin not, and yet I say unto you, that Solomon in all his glory was not arrayed like one of these."

Luke 12:27

The key-word here is "how." They grow in beauty and perfection because God provides for everything they need. Their roots take nourishment from the Earth; their stalks and leaves find sustenance from the rain; they are gently exercised by the wind. Their blossoms take their color and beauty from the very essence of the vital life-giver, the Sun, while their fragrance is bestowed by God Himself!

We can see the lesson here, and give our bodies what they need for renewal. Science tells us that every day of our lives many body cells are worn out and discarded, but at the same time new cells are built to replace them. The discarded cells may carry away negative vibrations, and even polluted matter, giving us the opportunity to renew ourselves with cells that are pure and good. The more idealistic and happy thoughts we entertain, the more we purify our cells. We really stamp the new cells with the Divine Pattern of spiritual consciousness.

The sudden rush of new information about the two halves of the brain has stimulated metaphysicians to think in terms of planetary relationships. Saturn (8), the disciplinarian, and Jupiter (3), the planet of the higher mind, have been known to be a tremendous positive power when in conjunction. The resulting combined vibrations often produce mastership in both the spiritual and scientific fields. History shows that Jesus, Buddha, Mohammed, Mary Baker Eddy, and many other religious leaders were born when these two planets were in conjunction. Numerological vibrations also confirm that the Saturn and Jupiter numbers 8 and 3, when combined, produce the spiritual master number 11.

It is believed that Jupiter rules the right hemisphere of the brain, and Saturn, the left hemisphere. The Saturn side of the brain seems related to the desires of the body senses for possessions, sensations, power, material success, and money. The desire of the soul, the Jupiter side, works toward love, beauty, rhythm, balance, and philosophy, plus an awakening within for happiness and harmony.

Present research also suggests indications that synchronizing the electro-magnetic energies of the right and left brain hemispheres can have highly important effects on personal creativity and invention. It undoubtedly will be found that telepathic communications among all peoples will be augmented far beyond present expectations.

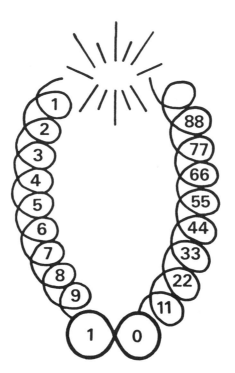

Chapter Twenty-Four

Master Number Eighty-Eight

Souls are glorified — or destroyed — by thought power. It follows that after gaining this spiritual atomic energy within, no negative vibrations can be allowed to enter the consciousness. Thought is power; it is under our free will to discriminate in our use of it. Planting a seed-thought is done by holding the thought with deep intensity until that thought idea goes into the realm of the emotions. When thought and emotions mingle, the seed takes root and expresses. Emotion gives it the necessary impetus to produce. The Life Force then generates it as a firm vibration released into consciousness.

```
MASTERSHIP DISCIPLE
4112591897 49139735
88
```

The master number 88 level of consciousness builds truth with honest simplicity. Here individuals get to know their inner selves and have positive urges as expressed in art, science, music, or literature, always in calmness and balance. To grow slowly and thoroughly is the responsibility of the double 8.

Consider the equation: 88/16/7. The equation for this "loop" of the seeker's spiritual ascent demands strict behavioral discipline. Subtly underlying the number 88 we find the malefic number 16 (8 + 8 = 16). This means that although these people have made the effort to reach the 88 state of consciousness, they are still vulnerable at times to their emotional urges. They need to be exceptionally watchful as situations arise in their lives where temptation is very hard to ignore.

The number 16 is a combination of the lovely Venus 6 and the flamboyant will of Mars 1. The determined nature of Mars demands response and acceptance, and resists being diverted from its amorous desires. The underlying digit 7 (Moon) is emotional and changeable as well, creating a combination of vibrations that are difficult for individuals to overcome. Mars is too much of a "live wire" to be content without close human contact, which often leads to unfortunate or disappointing romantic episodes. However, this does not preclude deeper love and marriage.

The number 8 stands for power moving in material form, or within people who are incarnated in physical bodies. A double 8, therefore, accentuates this power greatly. The number 8 corresponds to Saturn, the planet which is considered the spiritual foundation of a personality. Saturn is a planet of discipleship; it brings about opportunity through difficult situations and crises; free choice and correct decisions are required in order to produce progress. Through our degree of illumination, we see the significance of events old and new, past and present, and can estimate future results of our choices and conduct.

One becomes an initiate under Capricorn-ruled Saturn.

One becomes a world-server under Uranus-ruled Aquarius.

One becomes a world savior under Neptune-ruled Pisces.

Our bodies need rigid discipline to attain stimulation into spiritual actions. The nature of the flesh body is constantly at variance with the laws of God; in other words, the misconceptions of mass-mind (which is another name for Devil, or evil) rules the body and allows error to creep in. There is nothing evil in the flesh body itself, as mass-mind would infer. The physical body is simply the vehicle of sensing. The world's desires of the senses lead to answering the fleshly demands, sometimes to excess. We thus find in the double 8 the lesson of discipline for both mind and body. The downward pull of Saturn, as the planet of limitation and gravity, has an influence of binding us to materiality.

In *The Teachings of the Compassionate Buddha* we find the eight laws which must be followed if the body is to become whole.

1. Right body function — eating, drinking.
2. Right breathing — pure air, deep draughts.
3. Right thinking.
4. Right action.
5. Right humility — pridelessness.
6. Right mindfulness.
7. Right tolerance, understanding, love.
8. Right nourishment — in all ways.[1]

A higher body power is levitation. These ideas of the future seem somewhat like science fiction, but when we consider the potential of the two hemispheres of the brain when united, fiction could become reality. Our future exercises, instead of jogging or yoga, may be a daily practice to re-align our brain function for each new day's activities — a sort of toning up of the hemispheres of the brain to make available their maximum resources.

```
MIRACULOUS LEVITATION
4991333631 3549212965
88
```

It is not entirely new to be thinking in this way, for meditation has been taught in all ages, but now perhaps this process for exploration can be utilized in a different way, as new mental frontiers are being explored. The possibility of gaining more conscious awareness through the merger of spiritual ideals with scientifically developed principles seems to be the "in" thing as we proceed further into the Aquarian Age. The areas to be researched are enormous. Holistic healing alone opens vast areas for metaphysical research.

It is time that we acknowledged the fact that there is another kind of awareness in human consciousness, as a result of serious studies and research in the possibilities of human brain power.

COSMIC FORERUNNER
361493 6695935559
88

It is most significant that the words on the Great Seal of the United States of America are prophetic of this condition.

NOVUS ORDO SECLORUM
(New World Order)

Through the power inherent in this incarnation, we can gain great wealth and fame through our tremendous ambition; then we need to expand from the philosophy of material abundance to the philanthropy that benefits all humanity. Philosophical thought and communion with higher forces come during meditation. Spiritually-minded persons know that all they seek — peace, joy, love, serenity, and security — is really within, the gift of the spirit.

We should learn to accept ourselves, respect ourselves, and take responsibility for ourselves in the dignity of the human status, as an extension of Divinity.

The power and glory in the number 8 is doubled in the master number 88; thus, handling these vibrations becomes a challenge to our judgmental skills. The best choice becomes a study involving correct motives for long range or future outcomes. We must consider action that will follow right and justice for the good of all humankind.

Some of the great intelligences who were called upon to make important decisions in the past were philosophers and prophets, such as Lao Tze and Confucius of China, Buddha of India, Zoroaster of Persia, Pythagoras of Greece, and Ezekiel and Daniel of Israel.

Chapter Twenty-Five

Ninety-Two/Eleven: Testing Number

In our journey up the 11s and the double-digit spirals we have learned to cope with the many shades of testing, and have reaped many benefits towards enlightenment in the process. The soul has experienced various 11-type personalities, and faced and overcome many worldly temptations along the way.

Now we are reaching the ultimate in testing. We have come through Earth's material elements, its many highways and byways of distractions; we have met the questings of the mental tests with righteous judgments; and we have faced the often heart-rending emotional tests of evolutionary growth which the world requires of its citizens.

The testing number 92/11 vibration brings with it the challenge of the spiritual element: fire. The fiery planet Vulcan (number 2) working through the vital, life-giving energy of the Sun (9), which is both fire and light, will bestow on the testing number 92 person the baptism of the Holy Spirit.

"For our God is a consuming fire."
Hebrews 13:29

". . . He shall baptize you with the Holy Ghost and with Fire."
Matthew 3:11

> "We are concerned with the development of the soul body, which can pass unharmed through fire, air, water and earth on missions of love and mercy."[1]

Soul bodies can be strengthened through love, purity, selfless service, and good-will. Perhaps these souls began their physical "trek" in far-off Lemuria, where there was good-will toward all, where no violence was known and where the Divine Light was revered and worshipped. Perhaps they were souls who fled that continent before its sinking, and were members of the tall people who carved the following message into a rock at Tiahuanaco, which was occupied by a galactic race of superhumans who were seven feet tall. A huge monolith is found there with the inscription:

> "Sons and daughters of Light — believe in yourselves, and believing, reach out to the children of darkness whom you have come to teach and uplift . . . the Earth is the home of a race destined for greatness within the Cosmos, and your task is to seek ways to encourage them in the battle for individuality and Light."[2]

These souls' next lives may have been on Atlantis, where science was greatly advanced while spiritual growth became proportionately limited. People became more worldly, until, after many incarnations, the time came when the soul within began to realize that life was not what it could — and should — be for the further realization of health and happiness.

The axiom, "Change your thought and you change your life" repeated itself in these individuals' minds until they began to increase their prayers and meditations. This program started them anew on a genuine search for God. They listened in silence until the words they heard within their consciousness meant more than their awareness had understood; this became a most fascinating pursuit and led them ever onward.

They found in their search that the Holy Spirit is healing, cleansing, comforting, and balancing. The baptism of fire was working. They found also that the Holy Spirit guides our lives and brings harmony, peace, revelations, and — finally — illumination. The Holy Spirit is truly unlimited in Its power to bestow happiness and prosperity.

```
EVOLVING LIFE FORMS
54634957 3965 66941
92/11
```

The soul-steps here described become necessary to all those who seek to gain initiation into Cosmic Consciousness.

```
FUTURE POSSIBILITIES
632395 7611929392951
92/11
```

"The physical nature of man has not changed in eons of time, but in his mental development he moves forward day by day, thus in his spiritual progress the cycles of Divine Order are evident."[3]

David Wood

```
ARISE, GO TO THE FATHER
19915  76 26 285 612859
92/11
```

Luke 15:18

Notes

1. *New Age Bible Interpretation* (Los Angeles: New Age Press, 1938).

2. *Seasons of the Spirit,* Hilarion Series (Toronto: Marcus Books), p. 32.

3. David Wood, *The First Book of the Revelation* (Kent, England: The Barton Press, 1985), p. 71.

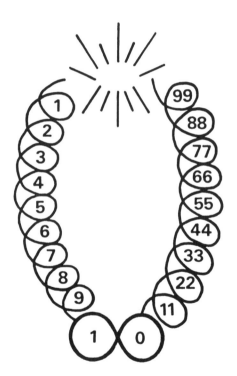

Chapter Twenty-Six

Master Number Ninety-Nine

Cycle by cycle, century by century, human civilization demonstrates a growing manifestation of Divinity, a reflection of the Spirit in all its glory. The 99 level of consciousness teaches health through universal purity, because we know that any physical malfunction will affect growth and attainment in a negative manner. When we are free from former negative habits and erroneous ideas, we are ready to become "one" with Cosmic Consciousness.

```
LIFE STRENGTH VITALITY
3965 12955728 49213927
99
```

We are evolving life-forms, instruments through which spirit seeks to fulfill its desire to attain reunion with God. We have an inherent ability — it could be said that it is our sacred duty — to restore our relationship with our loving Father, God. We create our own conditions in life and we are responsible for our own environment. God bestows the ability for revelation to all who seek daily guidance, through the Holy Spirit, as our Divine Gift.

"Seek and ye shall find." (Matthew 7:7) The only requirement is that we do seek and ask with loving motive.

To have a beautiful society is our urgent need. We must all have equal opportunity to gain knowledge, to have Divine guidance, and to cultivate beauty of soul. God, love, and truth are attributes of the same intelligent force; therefore, the consistent practice of love and of seeking Divine communion will help raise the level of consciousness.

```
THE AGE OF ILLUMINATION
285 175 66 933349512965
99
```

The age of Cosmic Love is here when we begin to give more than we take. One who knows love must give it out; love and light are one. The light of love is a potent force in the Universe. It is impossible to unfold without love. The search for love is the search for God. We must return to our Divine Center of Awareness in order to receive direct guidance into Cosmic Intelligence, which can lead us on the path of dedicated service. The higher the vibration, the higher our position in the Divine Order.

> "And now abideth faith, hope and love, these three, but the greatest of these is love."
>
> I Corinthians 13:13

> "There is no difficulty which love cannot conquer,
> No disease that love will not heal,
> No door that love will not open,
> No will that love will not subdue,
> No sin that love will not redeem."[1]
>
> Emmet Fox

It makes no difference how deeply seated the trouble may be, how hopeless the outlook, how great the mistake — a true realization of love will solve it all. If only people could love enough, they would be the happiest and most powerful beings in the world. Love begets love. When we project loving thoughts, we receive loving responses. Being a faithful friend brings devoted friendships; furthermore, love of humanity induces a sense of peace.

```
RESURRECTING POWER
951399532957 76559
99
```

By means of steady demonstrations of enlightenment under direct Divine guidance, we are capable of gradually eliminating much of human suffering. Concerted effort by groups of people in applying these principles makes it possible to eliminate much human misery. When we learn to live lovingly, misfortune will decrease as humans grow in heart and soul. Love is the best therapy. Love of liberty and human rights could form an alliance of world expansion — a common motive for the good of all. It is divinely ordained that in the New Golden Age love will reign supreme as humankind develops — although it may take many cycles to attain to that estate.

```
SYMPATHY AND FORBEARANCE
17471287 154 66925191535
99
```

Love is the long-sought-after "Elixir of Life" which is capable of transmuting pain to joy. Symbolically, the alchemists say it this way, "We can change lead (pain) to gold (joy)." With the present exploration of the whole-brain consciousness, a great awakening and soul-searching is occurring.

Education should open the self to inspiration with the Divine flow of creative ideals, and promote an exciting and thrilling adventure into the wonders of God and nature. All people have the seeds of greatness embedded in their natures; inspirational learning would lead to their complete mental, physical, and spiritual freedom. This would seem like the unfolding of a Holy plan, a development of spiritual sensitivity. This ideal can grow uninhibited in

```
THE UNITED STATES OF AMERICA
285 359254 121251 66 1459931
99
```

as our nation's founders envisioned.

A common language could be learned; there would be world literacy, with education for people of all ages, races, creeds, and colors. Each human being would be taught the value and development of Divine Love, for when humanity achieves the ability to function in harmony with God, it can receive impressions for better patterns of living, for promoting more desirable events, and for creating circumstances whereby all people can cooperate in harmony. A dominant pattern of total thought force that includes all humanity would prevail, as expressed in human events and in physical manifestation.

Our political system, if lovingly motivated and administrated, could bring enduring peace and success. This can work internationally as well, through satellite communication. Our United Nations could fuse into an International Peace Force for the whole planet. America could become a nation whose foundation is divinely guided, as our ancestors intended. A new era is approaching wherein it will be difficult to deceive others, because everyone will have developed the ability to "read" the thoughts and motives of others. We must learn to have dominion over

Fish of the sea (emotions)
Birds of the air (thoughts)
And all cattle (animal appetites)
And every living thing moving on the Earth.

We must get ready for new dimensions in consciousness. This ideal state must be part of God's Plan for us. Spiritual ecstasy, infused with Cosmic Wisdom, suddenly and completely becomes as a sort of omniscience. A clear, intelligent mentality, when fused with the numinous, produces an expansion of consciousness and a sense of Universality, with faith in the ability to accomplish the high goal of mastership, and possibly the added gift of the "miraculous touch." "Jesus touched Peter, and Peter was able to walk on the water." (Matthew 14:31)

```
IMMORTALITY EVOLUTION
94469213927 546332965
99
```

When individuals have reached and accepted an incarnation under master number 99, they know that they will have a "world" of vibrations to meet and experience. Consider the equation 99/18/9 by substituting planets and words as symbols representing the number patterns. (See Appendix A.)

Numbers	Planets	Keywords
99	Sun, Sun	Love, Love
18	Mars, Saturn	Energy, Discipline
9	Sun	Cosmic Consciousness

"Out of the raw material of the natural man, the Divine Man is unfolded. Out of the corruptible body of the natural man is made the truly incorruptible body of the spiritual man. This incorruptible body is sometimes called the "Solar Body" — it is an actual body made here on earth, and not in a far off heaven after death."[2]

Paul Foster Case

Some other possible patterns:

Numbers	In Numerology	Keywords
99	Love, Service	Thought, Sight
18	Awakening, Infinity	Pioneer, Responsibility
9	Rapture	Growth

LOVE	RAPTURE
3645	9172395
18/9	36/9
(a Nine-power word)	(a Nine-power word)

In constructing these patterns, planetary characteristics may be used to represent the numbers, or keywords of the power represented by the numbers or planets can be combined to make the patterns. The reader can carry out these patterns on all the other equations underlying the master double-digit numbers, heretofore delineated. Practicing with these number-powers and equations can greatly enhance understanding, as well as improve further use of number symbols in many daily life situations. Always use the positive meanings for a "lift" in consciousness.

GREAT PRIMARY FORCE
79512 7994197 66935
99

" ... the purpose of each soul's entrance into materiality is to be a channel of blessings to others. Not for self, but losing sight of self and giving that which is the greater concept of the relationship that souls bear to the Creative Forces ... "[3]
Edgar Cayce

HOLY TRANSFIGURATION
8637 291516973912965
99

The person who has reached the 99th degree is ready for adeptship.

Notes

1. Emmet Fox, *Power Through Constructive Thinking* (San Francisco: Harper & Row, Publishers, 1979).

2. Paul Foster Case, *The True and Invisible Rosicrucian Order* (York Beach, ME: Samuel Weiser, Inc., 1985), p. 53.

3. Edgar Cayce, *The Readings* (Virginia Beach, VA: Association for Research and Enlightenment, Inc.), 1604-1.

Chapter Twenty-Seven

The Journey's End
The Ultimate Number:
One Hundred

The 100 level of consciousness is insight illumination. All souls have to progress to regain the God-Image, which was One in the beginning.

```
AUM FATHER MOTHER DEITY
134 612859 462859 45927
100
```

In the beginning there was unity. All shared in the Primal-Will-to-Good; so, in the future, humanity will return to unity, and consciously share in God's Omniscience. The Twenty-third Psalm shows clearly that the soul needs to be returned to its original Divine Image. "He restoreth my soul." (Psalms 23:3)

Each person, made in God's Image, has a natural urge toward finding its individual self-hood, or the soul's identity with the indwelling Christ. An ideal pattern to follow is the Lord Jesus. When Thomas asked Him "How can we know the way?" Jesus said to him, "I am the way, the truth and the Life." (John 14:5-6)

The purpose of all religious and philosophical teachings is to assist in the expansion of consciousness into the ultimate reality. Cosmic Consciousness experiences usually come following an emotional state of love, joy, and peace beyond imagination. There may be a quick flash of knowing, like seeing the whole Universe revealed as a sudden illumination. The Cosmos is filled with all life, human and other, eternally One, yet impressions make us seem like separate individuals, all working for good. This type of experience could also be called illumination. The awakening soul feels that it is "in the world but not of it." Jesus put it this way, "I am not of this world." (John 17:14)

Each of us must come to know ourselves as spiritual in nature, "strangers in the Earth." We must strive to conduct ourselves as worthy of the Kingdom. Our destination is enlightenment. A sense of Deity in us has driven us forward from the most primitive physical experiences and adventures to the Great Work of building a pathway of Light from the dense material world to the Spiritual. We came forth from the Light and we seek to return to the Light. It is worldly to measure success in financial terms, but if spiritual success is our goal, we attain that only by doing what our spiritual natures require.

```
THE UNDERSTANDING HEART
285 3545912154957 85192
100
```

Honesty, helpfulness toward others, fairness, and justice for all represent qualities we must strive to bring into manifestation. Spirit supports spirit. There will be sharing rather than greed, cooperation rather than competition. With understanding hearts we will faithfully uphold our efforts by opting for right action. There are definite laws, both spiritual and material, plainly pointed out to us within the teachings of all spiritual leaders. These rules "dawn" on us in the form of inner guidance.

The regenerated brain is the fruit of the cycles of progression. Evolution is unfoldment to the extent that Divinity is finally externalizing. Without faith there might be doubt and confusion, but with faith and with God's grace, all things become possible. Although worldly pursuits could kill the body, "The life of the soul is in the hands of God." (Matthew 10:28)

As we become infused with the Golden Age Elixir of Life, we will realize that we are all Christs in the making.

```
AM I MY BROTHER'S KEEPER?
14 9 47 2962859 1 255759
100
```

The soul's journey makes life seem like a great adventure during which we can unfold our latent powers. We begin to realize that the same powers of the Mystics are "sleeping" in us, awaiting our awakening, and we may choose to take advantage of the glimpses of splendor we have seen in episodes of our deep meditation. We read in Christian Theology of the possibility that transcendental union with the Over-Soul, or God, is indeed our destiny.

"The soul of man emanated from God, and is of the same substance with God. The saviour, Christ, was of the same substance with God, the Divinity under another form."[1]
Albert Pike

"In the beginning God created heaven and earth and veiled them with His own substance. The Universe as a whole is formed out of the One substance."[2]
H. P. Blavatsky

"Take Substance and pull it apart, you have Energy.
Take Energy and pull it apart, you have Ether.
Take Ether and pull it apart, you have Love.
Take Love and pull it apart, you have Thought.
Take Thought and pull it apart, you have God!!!"[3]
The Golden Scripts

```
GLORY  GLORY  HALLELUJAH
73697  73697  8133533118
100
```

We have traced the soul's journey from the number 1, when we described its need, through hope, vision, prayer, and incentive, then on through its aim, emphasis, and practice, and finally to its triumph. We now find ourselves

```
ON  THE  BRINK  OF  A  MIRACLE
65  285  29952  66  1  4991335
100
```

We never graduate from the school of life; we are students to the end, and with our last breath we still can learn!

```
I AM MY BROTHER'S KEEPER
9 14 47 2962859 1 255759
100
```

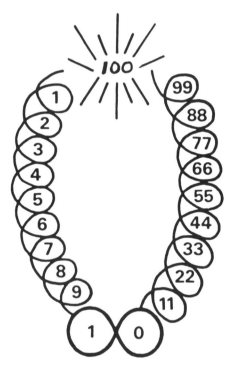

Notes

1. Albert Pike, *Morals and Dogma* (Supreme Council of the Southern Jurisdiction A.A.S.R. of U.S.A., 1871), p. 567.

2. H. P. Blavatsky, *The Secret Doctrine* (Wheaton, IL: Theosophical University Press, 1946), p. 326.

3. *The Golden Scripts* (Noblesville, IN: Soulcraft Chapels, 1951), chapter 57:7.

Conclusion

True, without falsehood, certain and most true:
  That which is above is as that which is below,
And that which is below is as that which is above;
  For the performance of the miracles of the ONE THING
As above, so below.
                              An Interpretation of the Emerald Tablets

My idea in writing this book has been to stimulate the search for God and to present ever-increasing cycles of Divine Order for the growth of consciousness. I have told you nothing really new — I have only helped you remember in your conscious mind the truth that you once knew, for you have lived many lives.

This book has been keyed to the symbology in numerology, which we can use for better understanding while pursuing development, health, and attainment towards a possible transcendental union with the Divinity. My hope is that in that union we can become co-creators with God and carry out the ideals which were ours from the beginning. These pages have been an attempt to present a "way" of unfoldment from intellect to illumination.

Thales, on being asked what God is, said, "That which has neither beginning nor end." He also said, "The most ancient of all things is God, for He is not begotten . . . and the most fair of all things is the World, for it is His Work." These statements were written five to six hundred years before Christ. What heights of unimaginable splendor lie hidden in the further future, no present half-evolved person can tell.

Human consciousness is changing, is attaining a higher level, and will keep on rising in the new Aquarian Age. God is the architect of everything that is, was, or will be manifested. This includes our Solar System, our Sun, the planets, the constellations, and every star we see in the sky.

We will learn not to go against basic natural laws of the Universe. None of us could survive outside of the elements of this present creation. A nuclear scientist looking at God in the Aquarian Age said, "Science seems to be on the verge of discovering God as a most fundamental fact of nature."

This book contains excerpts from notebooks I have kept over many years, yet I claim to uncover no new philosophy, but rather to present a pattern of thought that has developed over time. I trust that it will hold answers for some, even though it may sound strange to others.

"The most beautiful and the most profound emotion we can experience is the sensation of the mystical."

"The Cosmic religious experience is the strongest and noblest mainspring of scientific research."

"The Absolute is not an Earthly possession, it is a mission . . . and . . . each of us is a pilgrim to the Absolute."
Albert Einstein

When Einstein was asked whether he had to work very hard to produce his equations, he answered, "Oh, no, I meditate and the Numbers dance before me!"

I find the ideals contained in this book to be confirmed frequently in Christian teachings, as the many Bible references I used will attest.

I believe we are Divine Spirits with latent powers as yet undeveloped. Our physical evolution exists to make available opportunity for Spiritual evolution, and the law of justice governs this destiny. The result is a plan whereby we may achieve through our own efforts, whereby we may do "yet greater things" (John 14:12).

Strong souls are tested to temper them; weak souls are tested to rouse them; and great souls have to be chastened to become One. For only by the blend of strength and surrender, wisdom, obedience, and understanding can we attain liberation. This end alone brings peace within, the goal of all humanity, the fulfillment of the Divine Plan.

On this path to Divinity, we must learn to separate the "true from the false" by using our powers of discrimination. An ever-increasing expansion of our consciousness is possible. Serenity and stillness must be achieved to allow the reflections of the splendor of the coming Golden Age to appear on the mirror of our mind's calm surface.

There is a maxim, or principle, which says, "What you can conceive of, and believe in, you may achieve." The soul's journey makes life seem like a great adventure during which we can unfold our latent powers. We read in Christian Theology of the possibility that transcendent union with the Over-soul, or God, is indeed our destiny.

The ultimate purpose of this book is that we shall know from within, with ever-increasing Light and clarity. "Let that mind be in you that was also in Christ Jesus." (Philippians 2:5) We conclude that our minds and our consciousness is indeed unlimited. So, our field of study will be the limitless Universe, and our teacher the Creator Himself.

Appendix A

Those who want to learn how to find their own numbers and to understand some of the profound insights available through numerology may use the following number-letter code and keywords chart.

Number-Letter Code			Keywords
A 1	J 10/1	S 19/1	Activity, independence, unity
B 2	K 11	T 20/2	Tact, diplomacy, balance
C 3	L 12/3	U 21/3	Manifestation, understanding
D 4	M 13/4	V 22	Practicality, the builder, the worker
E 5	N 14/5	W 23/5	Intellectual, change, progress
F 6	O 15/6	X 24/6	Artistic ability, patience, domesticity
G 7	P 16/7	Y 25/7	Intuition, mystical ability
H 8	Q 17/8	Z 26/8	Ambition, effort, power
I 9	R 18/9		Universality, emotion, perception

Finding Your Numbers in Esoteric Numerology

The four major numbers derived from the name and birthdate are the Soul Number, the Personality Number, the Path of Destiny, and the Life Lesson Number. To find the Soul Number, add together the number values of the vowels in the entire name. The Personality Number is the total of the consonants. The Path of Destiny is the sum of the Soul Number and the Personality Number. The Life Lesson is derived from the sum of the numbers in the birthdate.

For ease in figuring a person's numbers, place the vowel-letter numbers above the name and the consonant-letter numbers below it. The vowels are A, E, I, O, U, W, and Y. Y is almost always used as a vowel; W is used as a vowel when you can detect the sound of it, as in the names Dwight or Gwendoline. (See Appendix B for further discussion of this.) In figuring the Life Lesson Number, use the number of the month born, the day of the month (without reducing), and the year added through once. That is, add together the four numbers in the year and use the resulting sum with the numbers for the month and day. When the resulting numbers are master numbers, the digits are not added together and reduced.

Example 1:

```
1  1   1 95 5  9 5      = 36 (3+6=9) 36/9      Soul
ADA MARIE WHITE                                Number
   4   4 9    8 2       = 27 (2+7=9) 27/9      Personality
                                               Number
                          63 (6+3=9) 63/9      Destiny
                                               Number
```

```
Birthdate: August 12, 1950
           8    12  15        (1+9+5+0)
           8 + 12 + 15   = 35 (3+5=8) 35/8     Life Lesson
                                               Number
```

```
5 9        1        5 19   = 30 (3+0=3) 30/3        Soul
DWIGHT MARK TWAIN                                   Number
4   782 4   92 2       5   = 43 (4+3=7) 43/7        Personality
                                                    Number
                            73 (7+3=10) 73/1        Destiny
                                                    Number
```

Birthdate: November 28, 1968

```
        11    28    24      (1+9+6+8)           Life Lesson
        11  +  28 + 24 = 63 (6+3=9) 63/9        Number
```

```
6 5      1 6       1   9   5  = 33 (3+3=6) 33/6  Soul
ROBERT SALOR GRANVILLE                           Number
9   2  92 1 3  9 79  5 4 33    = 66 (6+6=12)      Personality
                                66/12            Number
                                99 (9+9=18)      Destiny
                                99/18            Number
```

Birthdate: October 29, 1951

```
        10    29    16      (1+9+5+1)
        10 +  29 + 16  = 55 (5+5=10) 55/10       Life Lesson
                                                 Number
```

To find a signature number, vowels and consonants are not separated. The entire name is added together. (For further information on numerology I recommend reading *Numerology and the Divine Triangle* by Faith Javane and Dusty Bunker, Whitford Press, 1979.)

Example 2:

YVONNE H. DUDLEY
7 4 6 5 5 5 8   4 3 4 3 5 7 = 66 Signature Number

Astrological Correlations

The following table shows the number relationships of the planets and the signs of the zodiac. Do not confuse the numbers of the signs with the numbers of the months of the year when determining your Life Lesson Number. (For instance, Aries' number is 1, but the Sun is in the sign of Aries during March — the third month — and April — the fourth month of the year.)

Sign	Planetary Ruler	Number
Aries	Mars	1
Taurus	Earth	4
Gemini	Mercury	5
Cancer	Moon	7
Leo	Jupiter*	3
Virgo	Vulcan	2
Libra	Venus	6
Scorpio	Pluto	22
Sagittarius	Sun*	9
Capricorn	Saturn	8
Aquarius	Uranus	11
Pisces	Neptune	33

The elements — fire, earth, air, and water — are important divisions in astrology, but knowledge of them is also helpful in numerology. The following table of zodiacal signs, numbers, and descriptions of the energies of each will help you see how the two science/arts of numerology and astrology are related.

---

* I believe that this change in rulership of the fire trinity (the spiritual element) may be acceptable in the coming Aquarian Age. Here the Sun is placed at the pinnacle position until that time when the prophesied discovery of new planets will release the Sun (as the Power of the Zero) to take its rightful central position in the esoteric agenda.

Fire

Sign	Planet	Number	Description of Energy
Aries	Mars	1	The fire of youth, the instinct for leadership, dynamic energy for pioneering, "one who goes forth."
Leo	Jupiter	3	Idealism, courage, will-consciousness; mythologically, the Father of the Gods; the symbol of heart.
Sagittarius	Sun	9	Illumination, the Light of wisdom, the pinnacle of evolution, the "hope of glory." (Romans 5:2) "Light is the substance of Spirit, it goeth forth into all Eternity."[1]

Earth

Sign	Planet	Number	Description of Energy
Taurus	Earth	4	Material form, necessary for life on the Earth plane.

CUBE

3 3 2 5

13/4

The CUBE, symbol of the physical body, relates to the "city-four-square," which describes the developing consciousness as occurring on four levels of being: material, mental, emotional, and spiritual.

Sign	Planet	Number	Description of Energy
Virgo	Vulcan	2	Vulcan is an inter-Mercurial planet, associated with changes in the weather. It symbolizes selfless service, perseverance, tangible achievement, the dedicated industrious worker who makes practical use of knowledge.
Capricorn	Saturn	8	Responsibility, ambition, and business expertise.

Air

Sign	Planet	Number	Description of Energy
Gemini	Mercury	5	Symbolizes reason and the conscious mind.
Libra	Venus	6	Stands for art, beauty, love, and domesticity.
Aquarius	Uranus	11	Associated with super-consciousness and wisdom; (a higher octave of Mercury).

Water

Sign	Planet	Number	Description of Energy
Cancer	Moon	7	Relates to sub-conscious memory, and the emotions.
Scorpio	Pluto	22	Stands for redemption and the New Order; (a higher octave of Mars).
Pisces	Neptune	33	Represents intuition, mysticism, the psychic; (a higher octave of Venus).

Note

1. *The Golden Scripts* (Noblesville, IN: Soulcraft Chapels, 1951), chapter 30:26.

Appendix B

The Vowels

It is evident that spiritual evolution is accelerating; thus, growth in Universal Consciousness requires further power in the vowel sounds. The vowels in our names, as you recall, make up our Soul Numbers. Originally, the soul could be expressed adequately through the five vowel sounds — a, e, i, o, and u. These sounds represent the five developed senses of sight, hearing, taste, touch, and smelling.

Gradually, the vowel "Y" came into use, as a sixth sense — intuition, or second sight — began to develop. In about the sixth century B.C., Pythagoras considered Y to be a mystical letter and began to experiment with it. He took for himself a name (Yarancharya) with Y as a first vowel in order to experience it firsthand. (The first vowel in the first name is most important in revealing a person's main characteristic. If the vowel Y appears not as the first vowel, but later in the name, it simply adds to the soul vibration.)

In the twentieth century we have come to recognize that the letter "W" also has an identifiable sound vibration that definitely resonates within us. This letter has long been used after such letters as D and

G (as in the names Dwight or Gwendolyn), indicating that we have already reached the "edge" of the need for further vowel-sound development. The use of W as a vowel adds a double unit of higher consciousness to the soul's vibration, for it sounds like a "double U" in many names.

The sounds of the Y and W suggest that peak cycles in consciousness are occurring. The great universality of the letter W adds to our peace within, for it expands upon and emphasizes the vibration of the vowel U, which represents universality. Further use of the W alerts us to this power. Soul-sight and soul-hearing can be attained more easily as W becomes active as a vowel, for it stimulates the spiritual gifts available from the pineal — or master gland — to gather and spread its essence throughout our "Temples" (bodies).

Selecting a Name

We already know that the numbers of the letters in our names have much influence over us and, if recognized and properly understood, can be used as tools for personal guidance. Thus, we can use numerology to affect our soul development positively. Names are of prime importance, so we must choose them carefully. A name can be one of pride or shame; therefore, to be wisely named is to be greatly blessed and protected for the challenges we must face during a lifetime.

In selecting a name for the newborn, one must use understanding rather than sentiment for the name bestows an ideal vibration to which the child will respond. Each time the name is called, the individual will resonate positively — or negatively, which in time may cause him or her to seek a different name.

Many people change their names when they feel uncomfortable with the name given to them at birth. Some do this for professional reasons, believing that they can gain greater success with a new name.

Research and observation have shown that we are now ready for the full use of all seven vowels: A, E, I, O, U, W, and Y. We know that the law of life is progression, and that to stand still is stagnation. Let us not be afraid to grow.

Names with Vowels W and Y

5 1 7
D W A Y N E   first vowel — a triple (WAY)

6 5 5
O W E N   first vowel — a triple (OWE)

5 5 1
S T E W A R T   first vowel — a triple (EWA)

6
O S W A L D   first vowel — a single (O)

5 6
T W O M B L Y   first vowel — a diphthong (WO)

5 7
W Y N N   first vowel — a diphthong (WY)

5 5 5
L L E W E L L Y N   first vowel — a triple (EWE)

6 7
F L O Y D   first vowel — a diphthong (OY)

6 5 1
H O W A R D   first vowel — a triple (OWA)

7
T Y R O N E   first vowel — a single (Y)

1 5 1 9
G A W A I N   first vowel — a group (AWAI)

5
E D W I N A   first vowel — a single (E)

5 5 5
J E W E L   first vowel — a triple (EWE)

5 7
G W Y N E T H   first vowel — a diphthong (WY)

6 5 5
R O W E N A   first vowel — a triple (OWE)

5 5
W E N D Y   first vowel — a diphthong (WE)

Appendix C

Fasting: Preparing for the Challenges of the Higher Numbers

Fasting cleanses the body; it is a discipline for the mind and a dedication of the self to attain a goal. The time ordinarily spent in food preparation and eating can be used for thinking about spiritual concepts. A consciousness that is more highly evolved is a resulting benefit, one we should continuously strive to maintain. Moses, Mohammed, Socrates, Plato, Pythagoras, and Jesus are known to have practiced fasting for self-development.

> "On its way upwards on the ascending arc, evolution spiritualizes and etherealizes, so to speak, . . . thus, the nature of everything that is evolving returns to the condition it was in at its starting point . . . plus . . . a new and superior degree in the state of consciousness . . . . Everything in the Universe progresses steadily in the great Cycle, while incessantly going up and down in the smaller Cycles."[1]
>
> H. P. Blavatsky

Fasting promotes a general healing of the person. It gives the central nervous system a rest, frees the body of poisonous substances, and improves the defense forces of the immune system. And it renews the personality, allowing us to reform negative habits. Fasting also has an elevating effect on the consciousness and raises the I.Q.

> "During fasting . . . while the old cells and diseased tissues are decomposed and burned, the building of new and healthy cells is speeded up."[2]
>
> Paavo Airola

Fasting can be done for both short and long periods. A one-to-three-day fast can be helpful after a period of over-indulgence, such as a family festival or holiday feast. I recommend this simple, three-day fast: Eat only apples for three days. Be sure to drink plenty of distilled (pure) water during the time (tap water may contain chemicals or other contaminants).

The ideal fast, however, is one of twenty-six or even forty days duration, done under a doctor's guidance. (Always consult your doctor before you try to fast.) During any long fast, eat fruits only for the first two days, in preparation. All fruits except bananas are permitted. Apples, grapes, pears, pineapple, plums and many other fruits can make the period enjoyable. Drink plenty of distilled water daily. After the first two days, take only distilled water with a bit of lemon juice each time you feel hungry or thirsty. An alternate program for "juice fasting" is presented in Paavo Airola's book *How to Be Well.*

Breaking a fast is just as important as entering and maintaining one correctly. Don't eat too much too soon. In breaking your fast, drink plenty of grape juice; vegetable broth and V-8 juice are also good. When returning to solid food, chew slowly and thoroughly — the digestive process begins in the mouth. If you still feel hungry after eating, you did not chew the food sufficiently. Good fast-breaking foods include cottage cheese, baked apples, pears, peaches, and papayas. You may eat these with a little honey if you desire.

While you are fasting, your body will be doing several important things. It will use up any diseased cells it contains and will eliminate any excess fat cells which may have been a threat to your health. It will regain your natural contours, which you may not have seen for a while. It will begin immediately to eliminate the waste matter you have accumulated over the years. It will use the skin (an organ of elimination) as a means of getting rid of toxic poisons within; consequently, blemishes, pimples, liver spots, and small growths such as warts will often disappear. A faster's complexion takes on a fine glow and has the texture of a young child's. Its other eliminative organs — such as liver, lungs, and kidneys — will increase their effectiveness, both during and after the fast. It will normalize you physically, mentally, and nervously. Bad habits such as smoking, drinking cola, or even drug addiction can be broken. The brain and nervous system will function properly and you will feel invigorated in every way.

Will fasting make you sick? NO. Controlled fasting never made anyone ill. If, however, you have heart, diabetes, or kidney disease, etc., or if you have used heavy medication, you should not attempt fasting without the approval of your physician. And if you have discomfort while fasting, have a colon cleansing by a professional colonic therapist.

Fasting is educating the body and mind about health, and you will learn that you feel well on much less food than you formerly needed. Do not talk about fasting; it should be done as the Great Teacher Jesus advised his disciples: quietly and without "fanfare." While fasting, keep a calm and pleasant state of mind, and avoid worrisome situations.

What should you give up to have a sound and healthy body? It is recommended that you eliminate pork, fats, grease-soaked vegetables, and pastry and bread made from white flour. Do not use white sugar; honey is preferable. Steam your vegetables to retain their juices and nutrients. Eat raw vegetables and fruits, and their juices. Add many delicious salads to your diet. As an old adage says:

"The pleasures of eating are fleeting,
The pleasures of fasting are lasting."

We are not all alike, so our needs are different. Diets must be created to fill the needs of the person, depending on age, sex, previous history, and lifestyle. You can be your own nutritionist, as your own body will tell you when it is uncomfortable and will "suggest" what it would like to eat (through subconscious desires for certain foods).

Fasting is necessary for body purification and health. When a person is healthy, the atoms of the body rotate positively (clockwise). They manifest peace, health, harmony, happiness, and security. When diseased, the atoms rotate negatively (counter-clockwise) and breed destruction, poverty, disease, and death.

All things either evolve or devolve. Life is evolution. The goal of the Earthly cycles is the spiritualization of humanity. The awakening of the Christ spirit turns involution to evolution in the journey of the spirit through matter.

Notes

1. H. P. Blavatsky, *The Secret Doctrine,* Vol. 1 (Wheaton, IL: Theosophical University Press, 1946), p. 278.

2. Paavo Airola, *How To Be Well* (Phoenix, AZ: Health Plus Publishing, 1974), p. 215.

Glossary

Adept

One who has passed through all the initiations pertaining to the Earth Cycle and has attained the consciousness that will be possessed by the entire human race at the end of the Earth Period.

Akasha/Akashic Records

The book of nature. Space, or the recording ethers. "Nature's memory." Divine space. Pythagoras named it the "soul of the world." The Alpha and Omega of the records. "Ancient system of philosophy believed that the spiritual proto-types of all beings . . . were to be found in the boundless ether." (H. P. Blavatsky, *The Secret Doctrine,* Vol. II.)

Archetype

The original pattern, or model, of which all things of the same type are copies.

Aphorism

A concise statement of a principle.

Ascension	The process of rising upward, as Christ's ascension into heaven.
Aspirant	One who desires a lofty goal, as for an ascension.
Avatar	An incarnation of a Deity, or one formed by descent into human form from the spiritual regions beyond our life.
Centers (Chakras)	The etheric body contains seven centers, or chakras, which, when opened, give us exceptional sensing abilities. In the sympathetic nervous system, the centers are sensitive nerve clusters in the endocrine gland system.
Conversion	Changing from one belief or opinion to another. Voluntary change or acceptance.
Cosmic Love	An attracting, fusing, cohesive force moving toward Oneness.
Cosmos	The orderly Universe.
Cycles	Refers to series of events coming in measured regularity of ever-ascending spirals.
Death	An incurable weakness of corporeal beings, complicated in our world by the influence of an original "fall."
Disciple	A follower of a spiritual teacher, an Apostle.
Elixir of Life	Pure essence, veiled name for "birth of the Christ within."

Emerald Tablet of Hermes	The Hermetic science originally engraved on a tablet stone of Emerald.
Esoteric	Spiritual ideas beyond the understanding of most people.
Evolution	The progression of the ego through time, unfoldment to a higher consciousness.
Great Work	Relates to humankind's purification and conquest over self; to walk the "Path of Evolution" toward immortality.
Illuminati	Those who have special intellectual or spiritual enlightenment.
Initiate/Initiation	A beginning, entering on a new phase of experience, an increased degree of spiritual perception.
Involution	The process by which spirit enters into matter.
Kabalah/Cabala	Hebrew occult philosophy, mystical interpretation of the Scriptures.
Kundalini	Called the "fire-mist" which awakens the pituitary and pineal glands, which changes humans to super-humans by illumination.
Lay down one's life	Losing self to identify with the I AM.
Levitation	The raising of the body into the air and keeping it there without physical support. Said to occur in states of spiritual ecstasy.

Life Force   The "elan vital," the original vital impulse
                      which is the substance of consciousness and na-
                      ture.

Man/Mankind   Man does not always connote the male gender.
                      The word "man" comes from the word
                      "manas" which means mind; thus, man is a
                      thinking entity.

Miraculous touch   Said of Jesus: He touched Peter and it enabled
                      Peter to walk on the water. Also the "laying
                      on of hands" for healing.

Mystery   Refers to certain inner truths, not common
                      knowledge.

Mysticism   The more advanced spiritual truths.

Niscience   Knowledge. Having complete insight.

Numinous   The collective unconscious, the over-soul, the
                      Holy Spirit of Christian Theology, the Divine.

Numerology   A science of self-understanding attained
                      through learning the qualities of the numbers.

Occult   Hidden, concealed, secret, esoteric, related to
                      super-natural senses.

Omniscience   Having infinite knowledge.

Onomanics   Intuitive perception of the meaning of names
                      or words, the oracular use of numbers.

Philosopher's Stone   Veiled name for birth of the Christ within.

Rebirth	A method by which the soul evolves its latent power through successive manifestations on the Earth plane.
Sibyline Prophecy	Made by the "sybils" of ancient Greece.
Soul	The inner self as an entity apart from the physical body or outer self.
Substance	That which underlies life. Spirit clothes itself in substance and becomes form.
Urim and thummim	The means by which the high priest learned the Divine Will, through use of the "breast-plate" of Aaron, which consisted of twelve stones and their magnetic forces.
Vowels	The vowel letters were considered sacred, for they represented the "soul" or divine essence in names or words.
Volatilization of Matter	The process of turning substance into spirit.
Word	When symbolized by its component parts, the letter "W" represents a strong center of spiritual power. "O" is a focus of strong occult forces, a letter of transmutation. "R" is a symbol of universal service. "D" brings forth high spiritual forces into manifestation upon the plane of matter. These four letters carry the combined forces of the four elements: fire, air, water, and earth.
Yod	The tenth letter of the Hebrew Alphabet. A flame-like form, used in various combinations to produce all other letters.

About the Author

Faith Javane is an internationally recognized authority on metaphysical topics. She specializes in numerology, astrology, the Tarot, and symbology, and is particularly noted for her work in synthesizing these sciences. She has been a counsellor, lecturer, researcher, author, and teacher of these and related disciplines. Involved in numerous professional societies, she was a founding member of the American Federation of Astrologers and has also been very active in the Association for Research and Enlightenment (A.R.E.). She has appeared on numerous television and radio programs as well as at conferences throughout the United States.

Javane is co-author of *13: Birth or Death?* and of *Numerology and the Divine Triangle.* The publication of *Master Numbers: Cycles of Divine Order* marks her fiftieth year in the study of metaphysics. Her current projects include developing advanced features of astrology and preparing further thoughts on the Tarot.

Bibliography

Airola, Paavo. *How To Be Well.* (1974) Phoenix, AZ: Health Plus Publishing.

Bailey, Alice. *Esoteric Psychology.* (1951) New York: Lucis Publishing Co.

Blavatsky, H. P. *The Secret Doctrine.* (1946) Wheaton, IL: Theosophical University Press.

Bucke, C. M. *Cosmic Consciousness.* (1901) New York: E.P. Dutton and Co., Inc.

Case, Paul Foster. *The True and Invisible Rosicrucian Order.* (1985) York Beach, ME: Samuel Weiser, Inc.

Cayce, Edgar. *The Readings.* (Numerous Volumes) Virginia Beach, VA: Association for Research and Enlightenment, Inc.

Cheney, S. *Men Who Have Walked With God.* (1945) New York: Alfred A. Knopf.

de Chardin, Pierre Teilhard. *The Divine Milieu.* (1960) New York: Harper & Row, Publishers.

Fillmore, Charles. *Mystery of Genesis.* (1952) Kansas City, MO: Unity School of Christianity.

Fox, Emmet. *Power Through Constructive Thinking.* (1979) San Francisco: Harper & Row, Publishers.

Gammon, Roland. "Scientific Mysticism." *New Realities.* (1980) Vol. III, (No. 6), 8-14.

Haich, Elizabeth. *Initiation.* (1965) London: George Allen & Unwin Ltd.

_____. *Sexual Energy and Yoga.* (1975) New York: Asi Publishers, Inc.

Hall, Manly. *The Mystical Christ.* (1956) Los Angeles, CA: The Philosophical Research Society, Inc.

Heindel, Max. *Ancient and Modern Initiation.* (1955) Oceanside, CA: Rosicrucian Fellowship.

Heline, Corinne. *Sacred Science of Numbers.* (1971) LaCanada, CA: New Age Press, Inc.

_____. *Occult Anatomy and the Bible.* (1937) Oceanside, CA: Rosicrucian Fellowship Press.

Javane, Faith & Bunker, Dusty. *Numerology and the Divine Triangle.* (1979) West Chester, PA: Whitford Press.

_____. *13 — Birth or Death.* (1976) Hampton, NH: Association for Inner Development.

Joy, W. Brugh. *Joy's Way*. (1979) Los Angeles, CA: J. P. Tarcher, Inc.

Johnson, R. *The Imprisoned Splendor*. (1953) New York: Harpers.

Ouspensky, P. D. *The Psychology of Man's Possible Evolution*. (1954) New York: Alfred A. Knopf.

Pike, Albert. *Morals and Dogma*. (1871) Supreme Council of the Southern Jurisdiction A.A.S.R. of U.S.A.

Reyes, Benito F. *The Scientific Proofs of the Existence of the Soul*. (1949) Manila, Philippines: Lotus Press.

Russell, Lao. *Why You Cannot Die*. (1972) Waynesboro, VA: University of Science & Philosophy.

Russell, Walter. *The Secret of Light*. (1945) New York: Lecture given at Carnegie Hall.

Sai Baba. *Voice of the Avatar*. (1950) Andhra Pradesh, India: Sri Sathya Sai Books and Publications.

St. Theresa of Avila. *The Interior Castle*. (1949) Charlottesville, VA: Jordan Press.

Skarin, Annalee. *Ye Are Gods*. (1952) New York: Philosophical Library.

Starke, Walter. *The Ultimate Revolution*. (1969) New York: Harper & Row, Publishers.

Steiner, Rudolph. *Cosmic Memory*. Trans. K. E. Zimmer (1981) New York: Harper & Row, Publishers.

————. *The Etherization of the Blood*. Trans. A. Freeman & D. S. Osmond. (1971) London.

Taylor, Thomas. *The Theoretical Arithmetic of the Pythagoreans.* (1975) New York: Samuel Weiser, Inc.

Trevelyan, George. *Operation Redemption.* (1983) Wellingborough, England: Turnstone Press Ltd.

Underhill, Evelyn. *Mysticism.* (1955) New York: E. P. Dutton & Co., Inc.

Watts, M. *The Ultimate.* (1962) San Gabriel, CA: Willing Publishing Co.

Wood, David. *The First Book of the Revelation.* (1985) Kent, England: The Barton Press.

The Bible. King James Version.

A Course in Miracles. (1976) New York: Foundation for Inner Peace.

The Golden Scripts. (1951) Noblesville, IN: Soulcraft Chapels.

An Interpretation of the Emerald Tablets. Trans. Doreal. (1948) Sedalia, CO: Brotherhood of the White Temple, Inc.

The Kybalion. The Three Initiates. (1912) Chicago, IL: Yogi Publication Society.

New Age Bible Interpretation. (1938) Los Angeles, CA: New Age Press.

Seasons of the Spirit. Hilarion Series. Toronto, Canada: Marcus Books.

The Teachings of the Compassionate Buddha. (1955) New York: The New American Library of World Literature, Inc.